DASH DIET FOR BEGINNERS

THE BEGINNER'S GUIDE TO BURN FAT AND LOSE WEIGHT LOWERING BLOOD PRESSURE

SANDRA COLEMAN

Table of Contents

Introduction

The DASH diet is a lifelong well-balanced approach to healthy eating promoted by the National Institutes of Health that is based on nutrient-rich whole foods. This book will teach you exactly how to reach and maintain a healthy weight while lowering blood pressure and cholesterol.

U.S News and World Report chose the DASH diet as the best overall diet, the healthiest diet and the best diet for diabetes for four years in a row.

It is estimated that hypertension or high blood pressure affects over one billion people worldwide. Not only is high blood pressure the leading cause of death, it also increases the risk of stroke and heart disease.

The DASH diet seeks to reduce sodium in your diet and increase your consumption of calcium, magnesium, potassium and fiber by eating a wide selection of whole foods that lower blood pressure. Eating vegetables, fruits, whole grains, fish, lean meats, low fat dairy and healthy fats is all part of the DASH diet healthy eating plan.

The DASH diet is endorsed by the American Heart Association and is scientifically proven to lower blood pressure and cholesterol. Research has also shown that the DASH diet is extremely effective in promoting weight loss which has popularized it as a weight loss diet.

In a step-by-step way *The DASH Diet for Beginners Quick Start Guide* is going to teach you everything you need to know about how to successfully apply the DASH diet to your life!

Chapter 1 - What is the DASH Diet?

"Let food be thy medicine and medicine be thy food"
Hippocrates

The DASH diet is a well-balanced, lifelong approach to health eating that was discovered in research funded by the Nation Institutes of Health (NIH) to determine the role of dietary eatir patterns on blood pressure.

Over the years a number of studies have proven that the DAS diet is not only effective for lowering blood pressure through di but it is also effective in reducing the risk of cardiovascula disease, several types of cancers, stroke, heart disease, kidne stones, kidney disease, diabetes, heart failure and many othe diseases. The DASH diet has also been shown to promote weigl loss and improve overall health.

The Dash diet is recommended by:

The Mayo Clinic

That American Heart Association

The American College of Cardiology

The Dietary Guidelines for Americans

US guidelines for the treatment of hypertension

The National Heart, Lung and Blood Institute (a part of th National Institutes of Health [NIH] of the US Department c Health & Human Services)

The best overall diet

6

In January 2014 US News and World Report selected the DASH diet as the best overall diet, the healthiest diet and the best diet for diabetes for four years in a row.

The DASH diet was chosen by a distinguished panel of doctors for its healthy balance of food groups, its ability to improve health and its proven track record of successfully working time and time again.

Chapter 2 -Why was the Dash Diet Created?

DASH stands for **D**ietary **A**pproaches to **S**top **H**ypertensio Hypertension or high blood pressure has been on the rise in tl US for the past 50 years.

The continued increase of hypertension led the Nation Institutes of Health to propose funding for research that wou study the impact of dietary patterns on blood pressure.

In 1992, the National Heart, Lung and Blood Institute worke closely with five prestigious medical research centers in the US design and carry out the largest and most detailed study ev conducted called "The DASH study."

The DASH study was uniquely based on foods that the averaç person could buy at a local grocery store thus making it easy f anyone to implement.

The DASH study

The first DASH study began in 1993 and ended in July 1997. Th study compared two experimental diets with one control die Each of the 459 screened participants were randomly selected 1 participate in one of three groups. They were instructed to follo the dietary pattern of that group for eight weeks in which tim their blood pressure would be regularly checked.

The two experimental groups included:

***Experimental diet group 1** – Fruits and vegetables die*

Other than a high consumption of fruits and vegetables this grou was to eat the typical American diet with fewer sweets and snack Their fiber content was high and their magnesium and potassiu levels were similar to 75% of people in the US.

***Experimental diet group 2** – The DASH diet*

8

This group was to consume a high intake of fruits, vegetables and low-fat dairy. Fat content was low and protein and fiber levels were high. This diet was rich in magnesium, potassium, calcium, fish, poultry, whole grains and nuts. The consumption of red meats, sweets and sweetened drinks was low. (This diet intentionally included foods that would reduce blood pressure. It also contained a lot of antioxidant rich foods).

Control group – *The Control diet*

This group was to consume food that was typical of the American diet - low in potassium, calcium, fiber and magnesium and high in protein and fat.

The results of the DASH study

The results of the DASH study proved that dietary patterns *do* affect people with moderate to severe hypertension.

The "fruits and vegetables" group experienced lower blood pressure but their decrease was not as significant as the DASH group. The participants in the DASH group that did not have hypertension experienced a decrease in blood pressure as well.

The study also showed that people with hypertension in the DASH diet group experienced a decrease in their blood pressure within only two weeks of starting the DASH diet.

The DASH sodium study

The second DASH study called "The DASH sodium study" was undertaken following "The DASH study" to see whether the DASH diet could lower blood pressure even more effectively if it were low in salt. The two main objectives of the "The DASH sodium study" were:

1. To study the effects of reduced sodium levels on the DASH diet

2. To study the effects of the DASH diet at three different sodiu■ levels

The DASH sodium study was a large scale study that ran fro■ 1997 to 1999. It involved 412 adult participants with stage hypertension or prehypertension. There were two grou■ involved, the DASH diet group and the typical American di■ group (the control diet group).

Each group was given a 30 day diet that included three differer■ sodium levels: 3000 mg, 2400 mg and 1500 mg a day. Each di■ was preceded by two weeks of high sodium control diet eatin■ followed by 30 days of eating an assigned diet that randomize■ the sodium levels.

The results of the DASH sodium study

Both the DASH diet and the control diet were successful ■ lowering blood pressure at the lower salt levels but the bigge■ decrease in blood pressure was seen when the DASH diet wa■ combined with low salt consumption of 1500 mg a day.

The results of this study also led researchers to propose that th■ national daily allowance of sodium be lowered. The U.S. Dietar■ Guidelines for Americans recommend 2300 mg of sodium pe■ day or lower. 1500 mg of sodium a day is recommended for peopl■ who have high blood pressure.

Chapter 3 - Characteristics of the DASH Diet

The DASH diet is not necessarily a "diet" rather it is a way of eating that will promote long term health. The USDA (U.S. Department of Agriculture) recommends the DASH diet as "an ideal eating plan for all Americans."

The NIH (National Institutes of Health) says that the DASH diet plan does more than promote good eating habits. It offers suggestions on healthy alternatives to junk food and processed food.

In addition to this, the creators of the DASH diet say that "not only is the DASH diet designed to bring down high blood pressure it is also a well-balanced approach to eating that encourages people to lower their intake of sodium (salt) and increase their consumption of calcium, magnesium and potassium."

The characteristics of the DASH diet include:

Lower sodium intake

Increased vitamins and minerals

Increased good fats

Increased fiber consumption

Reduction of alcohol and caffeine

Customizable sodium and caloric intake

Lower sodium intake

The DASH diet provides guidelines for your sodium and caloric intake.

The standard DASH diet allows up to a maximum of 2300 mg of sodium per day and the low-sodium version of the DASH diet allows up to 1500 mg of sodium per day.

The average American diet contains up to 3500 mg of sodium per day.

Increased vitamins and minerals

All your essential vitamins and minerals are provided on the DASH diet by the many fruits, vegetables, whole grains and other whole foods that you are encouraged to eat on the diet.

The diet also includes an ample supply of minerals like magnesium and potassium that help to lower or improve your blood pressure.

Increased good fats

Consuming a lot of good fats and minimizing bad fats is highly encouraged on the DASH diet. Saturated and Trans fats should be replaced with lean meats, omega-3's from fish and seafood, low-fat dairy, nuts and seeds.

Good fats help to optimize our overall health by lowering bad cholesterol and increasing good cholesterol.

Increased fiber consumption

The DASH diet recommends increasing your fiber consumption by eating several servings of fruits, vegetables and grains every day. This keeps you feeling full and helps to reduce blood pressure.

High fiber consumption also helps to maintain good blood sugar levels and it also encourages weight loss.

Reduction of alcohol and caffeine

The DASH diet suggests limiting your intake of alcohol, soda, tea and coffee because they offer no nutritional value, typically contain a lot of sugar and they can elevate blood pressure.

Customized sodium and caloric intake

In the same way that you can choose a 2300 mg/day or 1500 mg/day sodium intake DASH diet, you can also choose the most suitable caloric intake level for you. The DASH diet allows you to choose a diet of 1500 to 3100 calories per day.

The caloric intake that you choose will depend on your weight, activity level, whether you have high blood pressure now or want to prevent it etc.

If you are overweight you will likely opt for the lower caloric intake level. If you are active then you will likely choose the higher caloric intake level.

If you have high blood pressure or are at risk of developing high blood pressure due to family history etc. then you'll likely opt for the low sodium diet. Consider working with your doctor to come up with the best combination of sodium and calorie levels for you.

Chapter 4 - Dash Diet Food Groups

The DASH diet is easy to follow because it uses common foo(that are available at your local grocery store. The DASH di suggests daily servings for each of the different food groups. T number of servings you eat will depend on your daily calor needs.

Have a look at the DASH diet pyramid here:

DASH diet pyramid

Please note: The daily servings suggested on the pyramid w vary depending on your calorie needs. You can find the require servings per daily calories in the next chapter on portion contr and serving sizes. *

Tier 1 - Water

The highest priority in any diet is making sure that you get tl right nutrients. A big part of getting the right nutrients includ(drinking enough fluids.

There are many people suffering from dehydration on a regul; basis because they simply do not drink enough water to keep the vital organs saturated with healthy fluids.

The perils of dehydration

The average adult body is comprised of 50 to 65 percent wate Fat tissue does not contain as much water as lean tissue so th more fat you have on you the harder it is for your body to stor the required water needed to help your vital organs functio properly.

With the body already being comprised of so much water yo would think that it wouldn't need anymore but that is not true. one area of the body starts to get dry it reduces the entire flow c fluids within the body. This lowers blood pressure by decreasin the volume of blood flow and it slows the blood pressure against the artery walls.

When this happens, a reduction in the amount of oxygen in the blood occurs thus lowering the oxygen levels that are reaching the vital organs and body tissue. As this continues, your whole system eventually begins to get unbalanced because it does not have enough water to keep the fluids flowing properly in your body.

How much water do you need?

If you are working out and sweating you need to increase your fluid intake to account for the extra loss of fluids. You should drink between 4-8 ounces of water during a workout every fifteen minutes and another 16 ounces after you finish working out just to compensate for the loss of fluids during a workout.

Our bodies need 64 fluid ounces of water every day to keep them working effectively.

If a nurse has ever had trouble drawing blood from your body then try drinking 64 fluid ounces of water every day the week before your blood work to see if it is easier for the blood to be drawn. 64 fluid ounces is equal to 8 - eight ounce glasses of water each day.

How to obtain the required amount of fluids

You can obtain fluids through other liquids besides water though not all liquids are created equal and some can actually harm your body if you drink too much of them. Alcoholic beverages or sodas are a couple examples of fluids that can harm your body. Milk, on the other hand is a decent source of fluid that can help keep you hydrated. It comes in second to water.

It is also possible to get some of your water intake from fruits, vegetables and the foods you eat. Watermelon for example is 90 percent water and can help your body stay hydrated.

The core of the DASH diet pyramid is water. A great way to mak your H2O intake more appealing is to add lemon to your wate along with a drop or two of liquid Stevia.

Signs of dehydration

If you go for an eight hour period of time without emptying you bladder, you are dehydrated. Signs of dehydration include dar urine, feeling tired, cranky, moody and experiencing headache. When you are dehydrated your heart also has to work harder t push blood through your veins.

Your body will react negatively when it has to compensate for lack of fluids so make sure to stay hydrated.

Scheduling your fluid consumption into your day

If you're like me, you might occasionally forget to drink wate throughout the day. Luckily there are some great alarms an applications online that can remind you.

Don't let a simple thing like forgetting to drink a glass of wate during your busy day cause you another headache. Get plenty c fluids and your body will reward you....plus you will be reducin the stress level on your heart.

Tier 2 - Fortified Cereal, Bread, Rice, Pasta

The second tier of the DASH Diet food pyramid includes fortifie cereals, breads, rice and pasta. Whole grain varieties of this foo group are best since they provide you with the most nutrients an contain higher levels of vitamins and minerals. They will als contain the least amount of processed chemicals like adde sugars and dyes.

But what do these foods do for you and how are they going to hel you in your weight loss efforts?

Grainy foods provide energy

The grainy food group supports your body's energy level as you exert force during exercise or when you use your mind to figure something out, be it a mathematical question or a personal dilemma.

Grainy foods keep you feeling full longer

Just half a cup of long grain rice included with a stir-fry can keep you feeling full longer than if you didn't include a serving of whole grains with your meal.

Eating oats for breakfast is a great idea because they are a great source of soluble fiber. Soluble fiber makes the bowels softer and able to move your byproducts along better.

Breads contain insoluble fiber and act like a bulking agent that helps keep your system regular.

Tier 3 - Vegetables and Fruits

The next group on the Dash Diet Pyramid includes both vegetables and fruits. The starchier the vegetable the faster it makes you feel full and the longer your feeling of fullness lasts.

The downside to starchy vegetables is that they turn into sugar when processed and often have less water content than other types of vegetables. Make sure to monitor the serving sizes and not make the mistake of eating too many servings of starchy vegetables.

On the other side of the DASH diet pyramid is the fruit section. Rich, sweet and delicious fruits can offer additional water to your diet. They also fill a natural craving we all have for sweetness.

Fruits and vegetables are a great source of phytonutrients and phytochemicals

Fruits and vegetables are a terrific source of vitamins and minerals that provide your body with the nutrients it needs to fight illnesses and rejuvenate your system. Your body's source phytonutrients and phytochemicals comes from this food group

Phytonutrients and phytochemicals are power nutrients th. protect you from hypertension as well as several other disease like diabetes, stroke, heart disease and some cancers.

Fruits and vegetables also help you maintain a healthy weight they lower cholesterol and blood pressure levels.

Eat colorful fruits and vegetables

Eat fruits and vegetables in an array of colors. Think "rainbow An acronym that can help you remember the colors of the rainbow is ROY G BIV. This stands for **R**ed, **O**range, **Y**ellow **G**reen, **B**lue, **I**ndigo and **V**iolet – all the colors of the rainbow!

The brighter and more variant the colors, the more nutrients yc will get from the fruits and vegetables.

Eating more than the recommended servings

If you choose to eat more than the daily recommended servin (see Chapter 5 for recommended servings) then it's best to ea more vegetables first then migrate to fruits, keeping in mind tha some fruits will turn into sugar in your body after you eat them.

When you are deficient in a certain vitamin or mineral there is vegetable or fruit available that contains the exact nutrient tha you need in order to correct that deficiency. Adding a vegetabl or fruit that you may not normally eat will allow you to cover a your nutrient bases so that you can correct your deficienc naturally rather than with a supplement.

Know how to cook your fruits and vegetables

Learning how to cook your fruits and vegetables in order to obtai the most nutrients from them is important.

The loss of nutrients during the cooking process can vary with fruits and vegetables. For example, cooking tomatoes is different than cooking other vegetables because the tomatoes nutrient values increase the longer they are cooked.

Other vegetables lose most of their nutrient value when they are cooked for longer periods.

Burning or cooking vegetables on high heat also causes them to lose a lot of their nutrient value. On the other hand, allowing a garlic clove or onion to rest a few minutes after it's been chopped can increase its nutrient value.

It's good to do some research on how to cook vegetables and fruits in order to get the most nutrients from the food that you prepare.

Tier 4a - Milk, Yogurt, Cheese

The next tier of the DASH diet pyramid includes milk, yogurt and cheese. It shares the level with meat, poultry, fish, dry beans and nuts.

The benefits of dairy

Dairy products are beneficial because they:

Help build stronger teeth and bones

Assist the nervous system in sending and receiving messages

Help muscles squeeze and relax

Help in releasing hormones and other chemicals in the body

Help maintain a normal heartbeat

One important mineral that is involved in all of these bodily functions is calcium. Calcium is a key ingredient in most dairy products.

Tier 4b - Fish, Poultry, Dry Beans and Nuts

The next tier of the DASH diet pyramid is the meat, poultry, fis dry beans, eggs and nuts group. This food group supplies the boc with protein, iron, zinc and some vitamin B and it keeps the bo healthy and strong.

Always choose lean cuts of meat and remove the skin from mea like chicken and turkey.

Benefits of this food group

Eggs are a great source of iron and protein so that's why they a listed with meats. Most of the fat in an egg comes from the yo so take that into consideration when deciding how many eggs eat in one sitting.

Beans are a low-fat source of protein. They also contain a hig level of fiber.

Nuts are a great source of iron and protein and they also contai high levels of good fat.

Tier 5 - Fats, Oils, Sweets, Supplements

The highest tier on the food pyramid is the fats, oils, sweets an supplements group. Each item in this food group is to be use sparingly. Opposite that is the calcium, vitamin D, vitamin B₁ and supplements group.

The DASH diet pyramid suggests adding calcium, vitamin D an vitamin B12 to your daily regimen because most people a lacking in these vitamins and the loss of these vitamins as we ag signifies the importance of an added supplement for thes specific nutrients.

Choose your oils and fats wisely

When choosing fats and oils you need to choose wisely. Omega-and omega-6 fatty acids are called "essential" fatty acids becaus the body cannot produce them on its own. You can only get the through food. These fats reduce inflammation and protect against heart disease. You obtain these fats mostly from fish, nuts and certain kinds of vegetables.

Processed foods contain a lot of fats and oils as well but these are not the best kinds of fats and oils to consume.

How much fat, carbohydrates, protein and cholesterol does that DASH diet allow?

Total fat - 27 %

Saturated fats - 6 %

Carbohydrates - 55 % of your calories

Protein - 18 % of your calories

Cholesterol - 150 mg

Chapter 5 - Portion Control and Serving Sizes

The DASH diet stresses the importance of portion size, eating variety of foods and getting the right amount of nutrients.

Often it is not what you eat that is the problem rather it is how much you eat.

Yes...measuring your food so that you eat balanced portion throughout the day of each food group can be a chore but it i important.

So how do you develop the habit of measuring out portions ever time you eat?

I started breaking down store purchased packages a long time ag and found that I actually repackaged foods in terribly larg quantities for mine and my families required serving sizes.

As I repackaged food I would tell myself that I had to make sure cooked enough and that I had enough for leftovers. Then I starte watching what we did with the extra servings that I ha repackaged.

Typically, we didn't use them for what I had intended and instea ate more than we should have.

It is amazing to discover that what you really need verses wha you actually eat are two very different things.

My husband's diagnosis as a diabetic slowly moved us into a nev era of eating in our family. His heart attack and insulin challenge which turned into our diet challenges became our main reason fo learning new behaviors.

Learning to read packages before I purchased foods became very important. Was the food worth eating? In what seemed like a day my value of worth suddenly changed. My eyes began to open to the importance of choosing high nutrient foods rather than foods that offered little to no nutrients.

I started measuring out snacks into portion sizes and repackaging them into Ziploc bags. This worked well because you didn't have to do the math when you wanted a snack. It was already figured out.

I broke down our meat packages into two, three and sometimes four different meal plans rather than making extra in one or two meals. I found that snacks were snacks and meals were meals.

There was a time when my husband would make a double-decker sandwich for a snack! Those days are behind us now and we realize that a snack is just that, a snack.

The best advice I can offer is to start your "portion size repackaging efforts" with the foods you currently have in the pantry, refrigerator and freezer.

When you start reviewing serving sizes there are some things that will undoubtedly surprise you about what a serving size actually is.

Learn about your foods and the processes taken to get them to market. You may find that buying fresh fruit and cutting it yourself allows you to eat more fruit. Why? Because processing includes additives that drive up the calories while reducing serving size. When fruits are canned they often require sugar as a preservative. This shrinks the portion size.

Also, when you purchase yogurt with real fruit the yogurt will contain additional additives that the manufacturer had to add to the yogurt to keep the fruit from spoiling. This is usually a sugar-based syrup of some sort. It's a better choice to buy plain yogurt and add your own fruit to it.

DASH diet allowable calories and servings

The <u>DASH diet plan</u> suggests the following servings per day each food group. There are three different caloric levels ; servings have been adjusted to suit each level.

1600 Calories a Day:

Grains (preferably whole grains or multi grains) = 6 servings

Vegetables = 3 - 4 servings

Fruits = 4 servings

Fat-free or low-fat milk and milk products = 2 - 3 servings

Lean meats, poultry and fish = 3 - 4 (or fewer) servings

Nuts, seeds, legumes = 3 - 4 servings per week

Fats and oils = 2 servings

Sweets and added sugars = 3 or fewer servings per week

2600 Calories a Day:

Grains (preferably whole grains or multi grains) = 10 - 11 servin|

Vegetables = 5 - 6 servings

Fruits = 5 - 6 servings

Fat-free or low-fat milk and milk products = 3 servings

Lean meats, poultry and fish = 6 servings

Nuts, seeds, legumes = 1 serving

Fats and oils = 3 servings

Sweets and added sugars = up to 2 servings a day but not require|

3100 Calories a Day:

Grains (preferably whole grains or multi grains) = 12 - 13 servings

Vegetables = 6 servings

Fruits = 6 servings

Fat-free or low-fat milk and milk products = 3 - 4 servings

Lean meats, poultry and fish = 6 - 9 servings

Nuts, seeds, legumes = 1 serving

Fats and oils = 4 servings

Sweets and added sugars = up to 2 servings a day but not required

So....what does one serving look like?

Here are some examples of what one serving of each food group looks like:

Grains

1 serving is equal to:

1 slice whole-wheat bread

1 ounce dry cereal

½ cup cooked rice, pasta or cereal

Vegetables

1 serving is equal to:

1 cup raw leafy green vegetables

½ cup raw or cooked vegetables

½ cup low sodium vegetable juice

Fruits

1 serving is equal to:

1 medium fruit

¼ cup dried fruit

½ cup fresh, canned or frozen fruit

Fat-free or low-fat milk and milk products

1 serving is equal to:

1 cup milk or yogurt

1 ½ ounces of cheese

Lean meats, poultry and fish

1 serving is equal to:

2 - 3 ounces cooked meats, poultry or fish

1 egg

Nuts, seeds and legumes

1 serving is equal to:

1/3 cup nuts

2 Tbsp peanut butter

2 Tbsp seeds

½ cup cooked legumes

Fats and Oils

1 serving is equal to:

1 tsp soft margarine

1 tsp vegetable oil

1 Tbsp mayonnaise

2 Tbsp salad dressing

Sweets and added sugars

1 serving is equal to:

1 Tbsp sugar

1 Tbsp jam

½ cup sorbet

1 cup lemonade

Chapter 6 - Dash Diet Food List

Vegetables

Low-Glycemic Vegetables (Make these your first choice)

Avocados

Arugula

Artichokes

Asparagus

Brussels sprouts

Broccoli

Bell peppers

Celery

Cabbage

Cauliflower

Cucumbers

Collard greens

Eggplant

Green beans

Kale

Lettuce *(the darker the leafy green, the better)*

Mustard greens

Mushrooms

Onions

Radishes

Spinach

Snow peas

Swiss chard

Summer squash

Sprouts

Turnip greens

Zucchini

Higher Glycemic Vegetables *(Make these your secor choice)*

Acorn squash

Butternut squash

Chickpeas

Carrots

English peas

Sweet potatoes

Spaghetti squash

Tomatoes

Not allowed:

White potatoes

Corn

Fruits

Lower Glycemic Fruits *(First choice)*

All fruits are allowed

Apricots

Apples

Blackberries

Blueberries

Bananas

Cranberries

Casaba melon

Cantaloupe

Grapes

Guavas

Honeydew melon

Limes

Lemons

Nectarines

Peaches

Papayas

Rhubarb

Raspberries

Strawberries

Watermelons

Higher Glycemic Fruits *(Second choice)*

Cherries

Figs

Grapefruits

Kiwis

Mango

Oranges

Plums

Pears

Pumpkin

Tangerines

Meats and Seafood

All shellfish

All fish (especially oily fish like salmon, sardines etc)

Beef (choose lean roasts and steaks and extra lean ground meat)

Chicken (skinless)

Eggs

Game birds and meats

Lamb (lean)

Pork (lean roasts and steaks)

Turkey (skinless and ground)

Turkey bacon (low sodium)

Not allowed:

Bacon (regular)

Cold cuts packaged and deli meats

Jerky

Sausage

Dairy

Almond milk

Blue cheese

Cheddar and cottage cheese (low-fat)

Cow's milk (1 % and skim)

Cream cheese (low-fat)

Feta-cheese

Greek yogurt

Margarine or butter substitute

Parmesan cheese (high sodium so limit)

Mozzarella cheese

Provolone cheese (low-fat)

Regular yogurt (low-fat)

Ricotta cheese (low-fat)

Soy milk

Sour cream (low-fat)

Swiss cheese

Not allowed:

Full-fat dairy

Butter

Cream

Fats

Almonds

Black walnuts

Brazil nuts

Canola oil

Flaxseed oil

Butter or Margarine substitute

Mayonnaise (low-fat)

Pecans

Olives (low-sodium)

Olive oil

Sesame seeds

Sunflower seeds

Not allowed:

Peanut oil, sesame oil and all other vegetable oils

Grains

Almond flour

Brown rice

Barley

Coconut flour

Wheat germ

Whole-grain bread

Whole-grain low carb cold cereal

Whole-grain mixed grain hot cereal

Whole grain pita

Whole-grain thin bagel

Whole-grain steel-cut oats

Whole-grain thin English muffins

Whole-wheat flour

Whole-grain tortillas

Not allowed:

Corn muffins

Corn bread

Corn meal

Oatmeal (instant or flavored)

Sweetened cold cereals

Condiments, Seasonings and "other"

Almond butter

Agave nectar

Coffee

Caesar dressing

Dressing (low sodium or no sodium)

Flaxseed

Flaxseed oil

Herbs

Spices

Hot sauce

Honey

Mustard (not honey mustard)

Preserves (low or no sugar)

Peanut butter (limit)

Jellies (low or no sugar)

Quinoa

Sesame butter

Salsa

Pickles (sour and dill)

Soy sauce (low sodium)

Teriyaki sauce (low sodium)

Tea (hot or cold)

Tomato of spaghetti sauce (no sugar)

Chicken, beef or vegetable broth (low or no sodium)

Vinaigrette

Whey protein powder (no sugar added)

Soy protein powder

Not allowed:

Alfredo sauce (prepared)

Cheese sauce (prepared)

Gravies (prepared)

Mayonnaise (full-fat)

Barbeque, steak and other sauces (low to regular sodium)

Sweet Treats

Dried fruits (no sugar added)

Fudge pops (fat-free)

Frozen fruit bars (no sugar added)

Gelatin ice cream (low-fat)

1 ounce square dark chocolate

Pudding (fat-free)

Popsicles

Sorbet

Sherbet

Chapter 7 - The DASH Diet and Weight Loss

Although the DASH diet was not formally created as a weight loss diet it does promote weight loss. This is due to the DASH diets food groups and guidelines.

The well balanced blend of nutritious low calorie whole foods helps your body drop unnecessary weight.

There are three things about the DASH diet that make it particularly great for weight loss:

Consuming healthy fats and omitting unhealthy fats

High fiber intake

High vitamin C intake

The DASH diet and fats

The average American diet contains a lot of unhealthy fat. Trans fats and saturated fats are extremely unhealthy, high in calories and have low to no nutritional value. They are the number one cause of weight gain on the **S**tandard **A**merican **D**iet (SAD diet). These fats are extremely limited on the DASH diet.

Healthy plant-based fats and omega-3 fatty acids on the other hand are an important part of the DASH diet and highly encouraged. Good fats are excellent for the body and the waist line!

The DASH diet and fiber

The DASH diet includes a lot of foods that contain soluble and insoluble fiber. A high fiber diet helps you feel full longer, slows the absorption of dietary fiber and sugar in your body an improves digestion.

This prevents blood sugar spikes while minimizing carbohydrat and junk food cravings. It also prevents fat from being stored i the abdominal area.

A high fiber diet is excellent for your overall health and weigh loss!

The DASH diet and Vitamin C

The DASH diet encourages a high consumption of fresh fruits an vegetables that are full of vitamins, minerals and antioxidant: One vitamin that plays a huge role in weight loss is vitamin C.

Vitamin C aids in the elimination of stored fat and it prevent hormonal reactions from occurring that can promote fat storag in the abdomen.

Problem is, vitamin C is easily depleted. Stress is the number on thing that depletes vitamin C. When your body is lacking vitami C it tells your brain that you're under stress. This causes a releas of the stress hormone cortisol that is sent out to store fat in th abdomen as a safety measure against the threat of famine.

If you can eliminate stress you can eliminate cortisol from bein released. Getting a sufficient amount of vitamin C in your diet ca also correct cortisol levels.

Having less cortisol in your system not only means a lowe accumulation of newly stored fat, it also lets your body know tha you don't need the stored fat that you already have. This equal weight loss!

Because vitamin C is a soluble vitamin that gets eliminated ii your urine it's important to eat a sufficient amount of vitamin (daily in order to lose body fat. The high consumption of fruits an vegetables on the DASH diet enables you to keep your vitamin C intake high.

Tips to maximize your weight loss

Choose low-calorie foods

You can lose weight on the DASH diet by eating foods that have fewer calories. The key to losing weight is to burn more calories than you eat in a day.

Exchange sweets and other high calorie foods for low calorie foods like fruits and vegetables. Eat smarter, eat smaller portions, eat slowly and be a smart shopper.

Low-fat frozen yogurt will save you nearly 70 calories when compared to full-fat ice cream. Buy low-fat or fat-free when it is available and cut back on portion size.

If you want a snack, choose fresh fruit rather than a cookie or candy. This will increase your fruit consumption and save you about 80 calories per snack.

Dried fruits are a better choice than chips or pork rinds and will save you about 230 calories per snack.

If you have to buy canned fruit make sure it is packaged in water and not syrup.

Plan ahead

Buy an assortment of vegetables, slice them and take them to work along with a sandwich. This will increase your vegetable consumption and it will help you resist the temptation to grab a bag of chips from the vending machine at lunch. Replacing a bag of chips with vegetables will save you about 120 calories.

Choose healthy snacks

Eat healthy snacks without adding unhealthy seasonings. T
popcorn cooked in olive oil and seasoned with garlic or grate
parmesan cheese rather than butter and salt.

Choose water

Drink water with a twist of lemon or lime rather than sodas ar
sweetened teas.

Adhere to recommended serving sizes

Watch your serving sizes on labels.

Consume less sodium

Sodium will make you retain water and it will cause inflammatoi
responses throughout your body. You need some sodium but ne
a lot.

Set a goal to watch your sodium intake and start paying attentio
to the information on food labels.

Prepackaged foods can contain excessive amounts of sodium.

Aim to buy foods that do not have salt added to them.

Note: Watch the salt content in canned foods, sauces, tomat
juices and prepared foods.

Be creative and exchange salt with exotic spices when cookin
meals. Let salt be your last resort.

Go low-fat

Choose lower fat methods of preparing your food such as bakinɡ
broiling and grilling.

Also, reduce the amount of oil and margarine that you use whe
cooking and use low-fat condiments.

Be smart about eating out

For eating out, do some research on the restaurant that you are going to by looking them up online to see how they prepare their food. You can get their menu online and find out how they cook their food.

Look for low sodium foods, low-fat, low calorie and special areas on the menu that offer lighter meal plans. If you do not see them ask your server.

Chapter 8 - Tips to Make the Switch to DASH Diet Eating

Ease your way into a DASH diet lifestyle by using these helpf tips.

Change gradually

If you currently only eat one or two servings of fruits ar vegetables a day try to add a serving at lunch and one at dinner

Rather than switching to an "all or nothing" approach to who grains, start by making one or two of your grain serving's who grains. Increasing fruits, vegetables and whole grains gradual can help prevent bloating or diarrhea that may occur if you arer used to eating a high-fiber diet.

Reward successes and forgive slip-ups

Reward yourself with a nonfood treat for your accomplishmen such as renting a movie, purchasing a book or getting togeth with a friend.

Everyone slips up sometimes especially when learning somethir new. Remember that changing your lifestyle is a long-ter process. Find out what triggered your setback then pick up whei you left off.

Make exercise an important part of your DASH die lifestyle

The DASH diet eating plan will improve your health and mak you lose weight all on its own. However, if you make regula exercise a habit you will boost your body's ability to she unwanted pounds.

When you combine DASH diet eating with a good amount of physical activity (30 minutes/day of moderate exercise) it will also maximize your ability to reduce blood pressure.

Get support if you need it

If you are having trouble sticking to your diet talk to your doctor or dietitian about it. They may be able to offer some tips that will help you stick to the DASH diet more effectively.

Chapter 9 - Tips to Lower Your Sodium Intake

The foods on the DASH diet are naturally low in sodium so you will likely lower your sodium intake just by eating the required foods.

Here are some other ways in which you can reduce your sodium intake:

Don't add salt to the water when preparing rice, hot cereal or pasta

Use sodium-free spices, flavorings or condiments with your food instead of salt

Purchase foods labeled "sodium-free," "low sodium," and "no-salt added"

Rinse canned foods to remove some sodium

Get rid of the salt shaker you would normally keep on your dinner table

Read food labels

If you are diligent about reading food labels you might be surprised when you see how much sodium is in processed food. Even foods that you consider healthy can still contain substantial amount of sodium. For example canned vegetable and low-fat soups are some foods that you wouldn't think would be high in sodium.

How much sodium is in salt?

One teaspoon of table salt contains approximately 2300 mg of sodium and a 2/3 teaspoon of salt contains 1500 mg of sodium!

Adjusting to low sodium foods

If food that you normally consume tastes too bland in the "low-sodium" variety then try making more of a gradual increase to low-sodium foods. Be patient. It can take a few months to get used to low sodium foods.

Chapter 10 - Dash Diet Seven-Day Meal Plan

Day 1

Breakfast: (442 Cal Total)

3/4 cup pure shredded wheat (125 Cal)

1 cup low-fat organic milk (100 Cal)

1 banana, sliced in the cereal (105 Cal)

1 cup of fresh squeezed, orange juice (112 Cal)

1 - 8 ounce glass of water (0 Cal)

Morning Snack: (200 Cal)

1/4 cup walnuts, chopped (200 Cal)

Lunch: (311 Cal)

Grilled chicken breast, boneless, small (141 Cal)

2 slices whole wheat or whole grain bread (85 per slice x 2 = 170

1 tablespoon Dijon mustard (0 Cal)

Salad *(29 Cal)*

1/2 cup cucumber slices (8 Cal)

1/2 cup tomato wedges (16 Cal)

1 teaspoon fat free, low sodium Italian Dressing (5 Cal)

1 – 8 ounce glass of water (0)

Afternoon Snack: (152 Cal)

3 tablespoons of yogurt – plain, nonfat (22 Cal)

1/4 cup of raisins (130 Cal)

Dinner: (645)

3 ounces of beef, top sirloin, about the size of a deck of cards (158 Cal)

1 cup boiled green beans (44 Cal)

1 small baked potato (145 Cal)

½ tablespoon extra virgin olive oil (60 Cal)

1 small apple for desert (116 Cal)

1 cup of 1 % milk (122 Cal)

1 - 8 ounce glass of water (0 Cal)

Total calories – 1779

Day 2

Breakfast: (377 Cal)

1/2 cup oatmeal (not instant) seasoned with cinnamon (150 Cal

1 medium banana (105 Cal)

1 cup low-fat 2 % milk (122 Cal)

1 glass of water (0 Cal)

Morning Snack: (160 Cal)

1/4 cup sunflower seeds (160 Cal)

Lunch: (617 Cal)

3 ounces of chicken in chicken salad (100 Cal)

1 leaf of Romaine lettuce up to 2 cups, cut up in salad (15 Cal)

1 slice of tomato diced in salad (16 Cal)

1 celery stick, up to 1 cup, diced in salad (18 Cal)

1 green onion, diced in salad (10 Cal)

1 tablespoon low-fat mayonnaise added to salad (35 Cal)

2 slices of whole wheat or multi grain bread (180 Cal, one slice
90 Cal)

1 slice of cheese (66 Cal)

1 cup of cantaloupe chunks (60 Cal)

1 cup of apple juice (117 Cal)

8 ounces of water (0 Cal)

Afternoon Snack: (152.5 Cal)

1/4 cup dried apricots (100 Cal)

3 tablespoons Greek yogurt (52.5 Cal)

Dinner: (356 Cal)

1 cup of wheat spaghetti (174 Cal)

1/2 cup mushrooms (22 Cal)

1/2 cup spaghetti sauce no meat (45 Cal)

3 tablespoons parmesan cheese (63 Cal)

1 cup spinach (7 Cal)

1 medium grated carrot (25 Cal)

2 tablespoon fat-free Italian salad dressing (20 Cal)

Total calories – 1662.5

Day 3

Breakfast: (449 Cal)

2 cups pure puffed wheat cereal (100 Cal)

1 medium banana (105 Cal)

1 cup - 2 % low-fat milk (122 Cal)

1 cup fresh squeezed orange juice (122 Cal)

8 ounces of water (0 Cal)

Morning Snack: (238 Cal)

3/4 cup Greek vanilla yogurt (170 Cal)

1/4 cup blueberries (21 Cal)

1 tablespoon sunflower seeds, no salt added (47 Cal)

Lunch: (460 Cal)

3 oz. grilled flounder fish sandwich (100 Cal)

1 slice of cheese, 2 % milk (45 Cal)

1 hamburger bun, whole wheat (200 Cal)

1 large leaf of Romaine lettuce (15 Cal)

1 tablespoon low-fat mayonnaise (35 Cal)

1 medium orange (65 Cal)

8 ounces of water (0 Cal)

Afternoon Snack: (308 Cal)

2 large graham crackers (118 Cal, each large rectangle or 2 squares is 59 Cal Ea.)

2 tablespoon peanut butter smooth or crunchy same amount of calories (190 Cal)

Dinner: (248 Cal)

3 oz. fresh tuna (118 Cal)

1 teaspoon lemon juice (22 Cal)

1 cup cooked spinach (41 Cal)

1 bran muffin (67 Cal)

8 ounces of water (0 Cal)

Total calories – 1703

Day 4

Breakfast: (404 Cal)

1 cup Greek yogurt with blueberries (80 Cal)

1 medium peach (40 Cal)

1 slice of wholegrain toast (69 Cal)

1 teaspoon unsalted low-fat margarine (45 Cal)

8 oz. glass 100 percent pure purple Welch's grape juice (170 Cal)

8 ounces of water (0 Cal)

Morning Snack: (281 Cal)

1 oz. or 24 almonds (164 Cal)

1 cup apple juice (117 Cal)

Lunch: (316 Cal)

Ham and cheese sandwich - 2 ounces of ham sliced extra lean percent fat (60 Cal) and 1 slice of 2% cheese (45 Cal) = (105 Cal)

2 slices of whole grain bread for the sandwich (120 Cal)

1 large leaf of Romaine lettuce (15 Cal)

2 slices of tomato (16 Cal)

1 teaspoon low-fat mayonnaise (35 Cal)

1 medium carrot, cut into sticks (25 Cal)

8 ounces of water (0 Cal)

Afternoon Snack: (139 Cal)

1 apricot (17 Cal)

1 cup low-fat 2% milk (122 Cal)

Dinner: (585 Cal)

Chicken breast skinless, boneless (150 Cal)

3/4 cup brown rice, medium grain (150 Cal)

1 cup green peas boiled in water (124 Cal)

4 oz. cantaloupe chunks (39 Cal)

1 cup low-fat 2% milk (122 Cal)

Total calories – 1725

Day 5

Breakfast: (669 Cal)

3/4 cup pure shredded wheat (125 Cal)

1 medium banana (105 Cal)

1 bagel (110 Cal)

1 tablespoon of peanut butter for the bagel (95 Cal)

1 cup low-fat 2% milk (122 Cal)

1 cup orange juice (112 Cal)

8 ounces of water (0 Cal)

Morning Snack: (94 Cal)

2 tablespoons of sunflower seeds, unsalted (94 Cal)

Lunch: (565 Cal)

2 oz. tuna solid white albacore (70 Cal)

1 teaspoon low-fat mayonnaise (35 Cal)

1 leaf Romaine lettuce (15 Cal)

1 slice whole grain or whole wheat bread (85 Cal)

Cucumber salad = 1 cucumber (8 Cal)

.....1/2 cup tomato wedges (16 Cal)

.....2 tablespoon red wine vinaigrette (70 Cal)

.....4 oz - 2% low-fat cottage cheese (102 Cal)

.....1 oz. almonds, unsalted (164 Cal)

8 ounces of water (0 Cal)

Afternoon Snack: (91 Cal)

1 cup low-fat yogurt strawberry (91 Cal)

Dinner: (551 Cal)

4 ounces turkey meatloaf (120 Cal)

1 small baked potato (129 Cal)

1 tablespoon 2% low-fat shredded cheddar (80 Cal)

1 cup collard greens (49 Cal)

1 small whole grain or whole wheat roll (114 Cal)

1 medium peach (59 Cal)

8 ounces of water (0 Cal)

Total calories - 1970

Day 6

Breakfast: (417 Cal)

1 low-fat granola bar - (110 Cal)

1 medium banana (105 Cal)

1 low-fat strawberry banana yogurt (80 Cal)

1 cup 2% low-fat milk (122 Cal)

8 ounces water (0 Cal)

Morning Snack: (160 Cal)

1/4 cup sunflower seeds (160 Cal)

Lunch: (404 Cal)

3 ounces of cooked chicken (100 Cal)

2 slices of whole wheat bread (138 Cal - 69 Cal ea.)

1 leaf of Romaine lettuce (15 Cal)

2 slices of tomato (16 Cal)

2 teaspoons low-fat mayonnaise (70 Cal - 35 Cal ea.)

1 orange (65 Cal)

8 ounces of water (0 Cal)

Afternoon Snack: (17 Cal)

1 fresh apricot (17 Cal)

Dinner: (395 Cal)

1 filet - trout, wild (215 Cal)

1 cup cooked spinach (41 Cal)

1 carrot (25 Cal)

1 small whole wheat dinner Roll (114 Cal)

8 ounces water (0 Cal)

Total calories - 1393

Day 7

Breakfast: (341 Cal)

1/2 cup oatmeal 150 Cal w/cinnamon to spice 6 Cal (150 + 6 C = 156 Cal)

1 medium banana (105 Cal)

1 cup vanilla yogurt (80 Cal)

8 ounces of water (0 Cal)

Morning Snack: (164 Cal)

1 oz. almonds, unsalted (164 Cal)

Lunch: (443 Cal)

2 ounces solid white albacore tuna sandwich (70 Cal)

1 tablespoon low-fat mayonnaise (35 Cal)

1 large leaf lettuce (15 Cal)

2 slices of tomato (16 Cal)

2 slices whole wheat bread (120 Cal - 1 slice is 60 Cal)

1 orange (65 Cal)

1 cup 2% low-fat milk (122 Cal)

8 ounces water (0 Cal)

Afternoon Snack: (182 Cal)

7 whole wheat crackers (120 Cal)

1 cup purple grapes or white seedless grapes (62 Cal)

Dinner: *(478 Cal)*

3 ounces blackened shrimp skewer - no salt (101 Cal)

Salad = 1 cup fresh spinach (7 Cal)

1 cup tomato wedges (16 Cal)

2 tablespoon red wine vinaigrette (70 Cal)

1 whole wheat or multi grain roll (114 Cal)

8 ounces grape juice (170 Cal)

8 ounces water (0 Cal)

Total calories - 1608

Chapter 11 - DASH Diet 30 MINUTE Recipes

The following recipes are taken from my DASH Diet Recipes book

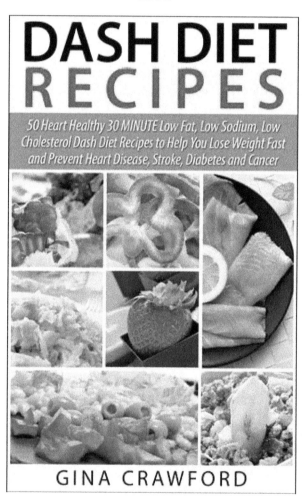

DASH DIET
RECIPES
50 Heart Healthy 30 MINUTE Low Fat, Low Sodium, Low
Cholesterol Dash Diet Recipes to Help You Lose Weight Fast
and Prevent Heart Disease, Stroke, Diabetes and Cancer

GINA CRAWFORD

The recipes contained in my <u>DASH Diet Recipes</u> book will help you maximize your DASH diet efforts and they'll take the thinking out of what to cook!

Pick up your copy today by clicking <u>here</u>

Breakfast

Raspberry Muffins

Raspberries contain a phytonutrient called rheosmin also referred to as the raspberry ketone (pronounced key-tone). Studies have found that this enzyme has the ability to accelerate weight loss. Enjoy this nutrient-rich, guilt-free muffin that tastes great and helps you lose weight!

Serves 12

Ingredients

Raspberries.....2/3 cup

Rolled oats.....1/2 cup

1 % low-fat milk.....1 cup

All-purpose flour.....3/4 cup

Grits.....1/4 cup

Wheat bran.....1/4 cup

Baking powder.....1 tablespoon

Salt.....1/4 teaspoon

Dark honey.....1/2 cup

Olive oil.....3 1/2 tablespoons

Lime zest.....2 teaspoons grated

Egg.....1 lightly beaten

Directions

Preheat the oven to 400 °F (200 °C). Line a 12-cup muffin pan with wax paper or foil liners.

In a medium saucepan combine the oats and milk. Cook (
medium heat and stir until the oats are tender and the mixture
creamy. Remove from heat and set aside while proceeding to t
next step.

In a large bowl combine the flour, grits, bran, baking powder ar
salt.

In a small bowl whisk the eggs and set aside.

Add the honey, olive oil and lime zest to the oats mixture and m
all the ingredients together. Add the egg to the batter. Mix tl
batter until moistened but still slightly lumpy. Gently fold in tl
raspberries.

Use two tablespoons, one to scoop the batter and the other t
push the batter into the muffin cups, filling each cup about 2/
full.

Bake until the tops are golden brown, about 16 to 18 minutes. Yc
should be able to insert a toothpick through the center and hav
it come out clean. If dough sticks to the toothpick, return tl
muffins to the oven for another minute or two.

Transfer the muffins to a wire rack and let them cool completel
before serving.

Nutritional analysis per serving

Serving size: 1 muffin

Total carbohydrate 27 g

Dietary fiber 2 g

Sodium 126 mg

Saturated fat 0.5 g

Total fat 5 g

Trans fat <0.5

Cholesterol 16 mg

Protein 3 g

Monounsaturated fat 3 g

Calories 165

Sugars 11 g

Buckwheat Pancakes with Strawberries

Buckwheat is actually a fruit seed and not a cereal grain. It related to the rhubarb and sorrel family which makes it a gre substitute for people who have allergies to wheat or oth grains.

Serves 6

Ingredients

Egg whites.....2

Olive oil.....1 tablespoon

Fat-free milk.....1/2 cup

All purpose flour.....1/2 cup

Buckwheat flour.....1/2 cup

Baking powder.....1 tablespoon

Sparkling water.....1/2 cup

Fresh strawberries.....3 cups sliced

Directions

In a large bowl whisk together the egg whites, olive oil and milk

In another bowl combine the all-purpose flour, buckwheat flot and baking powder and mix thoroughly.

Slowly add the dry ingredients to the egg white mixture as yo alternately add the sparkling water. Make sure to mix betwee each addition until all the ingredients combine into a batter.

Place a nonstick frying pan or griddle over medium heat. Spoon 1/2 cup of the pancake batter into the pan. Cook until the top surface of the pancake bubbles and the edges turn lightly brown, about 2 minutes. Flip and cook until the bottom is nicely brown and cooked through, 1 to 2 minutes longer. Repeat with the remaining pancake batter.

Transfer the pancakes to individual plates. Top each with 1/2 cup sliced strawberries. Serve.

Nutritional analysis per serving

Serving size: 1 pancake

Total carbohydrate 24 g

Dietary fiber 3 g

Sodium 150 mg

Saturated fat - trace

Total fat 3 g

Cholesterol - trace

Protein 5 g

Monounsaturated fat 2 g

Calories 143

Lunch

Sun-Dried Tomato Basil Pizza

Sun-dried tomatoes have high levels of antioxidants, lycopene and vitamin C. They are often used for tomato paste and tomato purees. The red plum tomato is used for sun-dried products.

Serves 4

Ingredients

12 inch prepared pizza crust purchased or made from mix.....1 crust

Garlic cloves.....4

Fat-free ricotta cheese.....1/2 cup

Dry packed sun-dried tomatoes.....1/2 cup chopped

Dried basil.....2 teaspoons

Thyme.....1 teaspoon

Red pepper flakes

Parmesan cheese

Directions

Preheat the oven to 475 °F (250 °C).

Lightly coat a 12-inch round pizza pie baking pan with cooking spray.

Sun-dried tomatoes need to be reconstituted before using. Place them in a bowl and pour boiled water over them until they are covered in water. Let stand for 5 minutes or until soft and pliable. Drain and chop.

Place the pizza crust in a round pizza pie-baking pan. Arran; garlic, cheese and tomatoes on top of the pizza crust. Sprink basil and thyme evenly over the pizza.

Bake on the lowest rack of the oven until the pizza crust tur» brown and the toppings are hot, about 20 minutes.

Cut the pizza into eight even slices and serve immediately.

Place the red-flaked pepper jar and the parmesan jar out f(individual use.

Nutritional analysis per serving

Serving size: 2 slices

Total fat 2 g

Calories 179

Protein 8 g

Cholesterol 8 mg

Total carbohydrate 32 g

Dietary fiber 2 g

Monounsaturated fat 0.5 g

Saturated fat - trace

Sodium 276 mg

Chicken in White Wine and Mushroom Sauce

Chicken is a great source of protein. For every 100 grams of chicken you get 30 grams of protein. In comparison, for every 100 grams of tuna, salmon and halibut there are 26 grams of protein.

This tasty dish is great when served over pasta. Add a side of freshly steamed vegetables for a nutrient rich, delicious meal.

Serves 4

Ingredients

Boneless skinless chicken breast.....4 - 4 ounces each

Olive oil.....2 tablespoons

Shallots.....4 thinly sliced

Fresh mushrooms.....1/4 pound thinly sliced

All-purpose (plain) flour.....1 tablespoon

White wine.....1/4 cup

Chicken stock.....1/2 cup low sodium

Fresh rosemary.....1 tablespoon (or 1 teaspoon dried rosemary)

Fresh parsley.....2 tablespoons chopped

Directions

Place the chicken breasts in a sealed Ziploc bag and pound with a mallet or use a rolling pin to flatten.

Remove chicken and cut each piece in half lengthwise. Return Ziploc bag and refrigerate until firm.

When chicken is firm, get two frying pans ready to cook by placing one teaspoon of olive oil in each pan.

In a small bowl add the flour and wine then whisk until all the flour lumps are gone. Set to the side.

Turn both of the frying pans to medium heat. In frying pan number one add the chicken breast. In frying pan two sauté the shallots for about 3 minutes.

Return to frying pan number one and turn the chicken breast over.

Go back to frying pan number two and add the mushrooms to the shallots. Stir while the two sauté together for another 2 minutes.

Get the bowl of mixed flour and wine. Whisk a few times and pour over the mushrooms and shallots. Add the chicken stock and stir.

The chicken in the first pan should be a nice shade of brown on each side and cooked through with no pink remaining. Remove from heat and plate.

Go back to the mushroom and shallot pan and stir, making sure it has thickened nicely. Turn off the burner and spoon mixture over the chicken.

Sprinkle with parsley and serve piping hot.

Nutritional analysis per serving

Serving size: 2 chicken breast halves

Total fat 9 g

Calories 239

Protein 28 g

Cholesterol 66 mg

Total carbohydrate 6 g

Dietary fiber 0.5 g

Monounsaturated fat 5 g

Saturated fat 1 g

Sodium 98 mg

Dinner

Balsamic Chicken Salad with Pineapple

The chicken in this dish provides a great source of protein while the pineapple contains free radicals that fight colds, strengthen bones and improve gums. Pineapple also has anti-inflammatory properties as well as antioxidants for a healthy heart. The nutritional value of pineapple also includes immunity-boosting vitamin C as it prevents hypertension.

Serves 8

Ingredients

Chicken breast..... 4 boneless, skinless - each about 5 ounces

Olive oil.....1 tablespoon

Unsweetened pineapple chunks.....1-8 ounce can drained except for 2 tablespoons of juice

Broccoli florets.....2 cups

Fresh baby spinach leaves.....4 cups

Red onions.....1/2 cup thinly sliced

For vinaigrette:

Olive oil.....1/4 cup

Balsamic vinegar.....2 tablespoons

Sugar.....2 teaspoons

Cinnamon.....1/4 teaspoon

Directions

Heat the oil in a large nonstick frying pan on medium heat.

Cut each chicken breast into cubes.

Add the chicken to the heated olive oil and cook until golde brown, about 10 minutes.

In a large serving bowl combine the cooked chicken, slice onions, pineapple chunks, broccoli and spinach.

Vinaigrette:

Whisk together the olive oil, vinegar and reserved pineapple juic Add the sugar and cinnamon. Mix together then pour over tl salad and gently toss to coat evenly. Serve immediately.

Nutritional analysis per serving

Total carbohydrate 8 g

Dietary fiber 2 g

Sodium 75 mg

Saturated fat 1 g

Total fat 9 g

Cholesterol 41 mg

Protein 17 g

Monounsaturated fat 6 g

Calories 181

Roasted Salmon with Chives and Tarragon

Salmon contains B3, B6, B12 selenium, protein, phosphorus, choline, pantothenic acid, biotin, and potassium. These nutrients are all essential for a healthy cardiovascular system, healthy joints, eye health and a decreased risk of cancer.

Serves 2

Ingredients

Organic salmon with skin.....2 - 5 ounce pieces

Extra virgin olive oil.....2 teaspoons

Chives.....1 tablespoon chopped

Fresh tarragon leaves.....1 teaspoon

Cooking spray

Directions

Preheat the oven to 475 °F (250 °C).

Line a baking sheet with foil and light cooking spray.

Rub salmon all over with 2 teaspoons of extra virgin olive oil.

Roast skin side down about 12 minutes or until fish is thoroughly cooked.

Use a metal spatula to lift the salmon off the skin. Place salmon on serving plate. Discard skin. Sprinkle salmon with herbs and serve.

Nutritional analysis per serving

85

Total carbohydrate - trace

Dietary fiber - trace

Sodium 62 mg

Saturated fat 2 g

Total fat 14 g

Cholesterol 78 mg

Protein 28 g

Monounsaturated fat 7 g

Calories 241

Salads

Asian-Style Vegetable Salad

Bok Choy contains more beta-carotene and vitamin A than an *other variety of cabbage.*

Carrots are great at reducing the risk of cardiovascular diseas *We typically associate carrots with the color "orange" but the* *actually come in fifteen different colors!*

It is recommended that we eat richly colored vegetables. Re *cabbage is a perfect example of a vegetable that has an intens* *vibrant color. The red pigment intensifies the vegetabl* *antioxidants and anti-inflammatory properties.*

Serves 4

Ingredients

Carrot.....1/2 cup grated

Red bell pepper.....1/2 cup chopped

Bok Choy.....1 ½ cup chopped

Yellow onion.....1/2 cup sliced

Red cabbage.....1 cup sliced

Spinach.....1 ½ cups

Garlic.....1 tablespoon minced

Cilantro.....1 tablespoon chopped

Cashews.....1 ½ tablespoon

Snow peas.....1 ½ cups

Low sodium soy sauce.....2 teaspoons

Directions

Rinse all the vegetables under cold running water then strain.

Cut the carrots, bell peppers, Bok Choy and yellow onion into thin strips.

To cut the cabbage and spinach put the knife across the grain and slice into narrow thin strips.

Mince the garlic. Cut the cilantro and cashews into slightly larger pieces.

Place cabbage, spinach, cilantro, cashews and snow peas in a large bowl. Drizzle with soy sauce. Toss well to combine. Serve.

Nutritional analysis per serving

Serving size: About 2 cups

Total carbohydrate 14 g

Dietary fiber 4 g

Sodium 173 mg

Saturated fat 1 g

Total fat 4 g

Trans fat 0 g

Cholesterol 0 mg

Protein 3 g

Monounsaturated fat 2 g

Simple Mango Salad

Mangos help to fight against different types of cancers. The contain vitamin A, beta-carotene, alpha-carotene, bet cryptoxanthin, potassium, vitamin B6, C, E and copper.

You can serve this salad over roasted chicken, chicken sala oriental vegetables, tortellini salads or any salad that can use little pizzazz!

Serves 6

Ingredients

Mangos.....3 pitted and cubed

Lime.....1 juiced

Red onion.....1 teaspoon minced

Jalapeno pepper.....1/2 seeded and minced

Directions

Combine all the ingredients in a mixing bowl. Cover and place i the refrigerator for 10 minutes. Toss just before serving.

Nutritional analysis per serving

Total carbohydrate 19 g

Dietary fiber 2 g

Sodium 10 mg

Saturated fat - trace

Total fat trace

Cholesterol 0 mg

Protein 1 g

Monounsaturated fat - trace

Calories 75

Appetizers

Tomato Basil Bruschetta

Tomatoes are a terrific choice if you are trying to lose weight. They are also beneficial in cancer prevention. One interesting thing about the tomato is that the more you cook it the higher the nutrient value climbs. Most fruits and vegetables lose their full level of nutritional value when cooked for longer periods but not the tomato!

Serves 6

Ingredients

Whole grain baguette.....1/2 cut into six 1/2 inch thick diagonal slices

Fresh basil......2 tablespoons chopped

Fresh parsley.....1 tablespoon chopped

Garlic cloves.....2 minced

Tomatoes.....3 diced

Fennel.....1/2 cup diced

Olive oil.....1 teaspoon

Balsamic vinegar.....2 teaspoons

Freshly ground black pepper.....1 teaspoon

Parmesan cheese......3 tablespoons

Directions

Dice the tomatoes and place them in a medium bowl. Add chopped basil, parsley, minced garlic, diced fennel, olive oil, balsamic vinegar and black pepper. Stir. Place in the refrigerator for 20 minutes to let the flavors blend.

Preheat the oven to 400 °F (200 °C).

Take the whole grain baguette and cut it into thick diagonal slice about 1/2 inch thick. Set on a baking sheet and put it into th oven. Toast the baguettes until they are lightly browned. Sprink with parmesan cheese while hot out of the oven. Transfer to salsa serving platter.

Add the tomato basil mixture to the platter in a serving bowl wit a spoon. Serve immediately.

Nutritional analysis per serving

Serving size: 1 slice

Total carbohydrate 20 g

Dietary fiber 4 g

Sodium 123 mg

Saturated fat < 0.5 g

Total fat 2 g

Trans fat 0 g

Cholesterol 0 mg

Protein 3 g

Monounsaturated fat 1 g

Calories 110

Sugars 0 g

Fruit Kebabs with Lemony Lime Dip

Pineapples have numerous benefits. They prevent free radicals from forming, they have anti-inflammatory and anti-cancer benefits and they help to prevent atherosclerosis.

Strawberries are full of nutrients and can decrease the risk of developing Type-2 diabetes.

Kiwi has phytonutrients that protect DNA. Kiwi is also a good source of fiber as well as other nutrients.

Potassium is a well-known benefit of the banana.

Red grapes offer a whole list of heart-healthy nutrients that include lowering blood pressure and cholesterol levels.

Serves 2

Ingredients

Low-fat sugar-free lemon yogurt.....4 ounces

Lime.....1 for 1 teaspoon lime juice

Lime zest.....1 teaspoon

Pineapple chunks.....4 to 6

Kiwi.....1 peeled and diced

Banana.....1/2 cut into 1/2-inch chunks

Red grapes.....4 to 6

Wooden skewers.....4

Directions

In a small bowl whisk together the lemon yogurt, lime juice ar lime zest. Cover and refrigerate to allow the flavors to marina as you prepare the rest of the recipe.

Thread one of each fruit onto a skewer. Repeat with the oth skewers until the fruit is gone. Since Kiwi acts as a natur tenderizer place it next to the pineapple or grapes and avo setting it right next to the banana to prevent premature brownin

Serve with the lemony lime dip.

To prevent fruit from browning, dip it in pineapple or oran juice.

Nutritional analysis per serving

Serving size: 2 fruit kebabs

Total fat 1 g

Calories 160

Protein 4 g

Cholesterol 4 mg

Total carbohydrate 36 g

Dietary fiber 4 g

Monounsaturated fat - trace

Saturated fat < 1 g

Sodium 45 mg

Sauces, Dressings and Dips

Artichoke Dip

Artichokes are great for calming the stomach or relieving stomach pains. Research has also found that artichokes can help reduce high cholesterol. If you have gallstones check with your doctor before eating artichokes. If you have allergies to ragweed, chrysanthemums, marigolds or daises you should check with your doctor as well since artichokes come from the same family of flowers.

Serves 8

Ingredients

Artichoke hearts.....2 cups

Spinach.....4 cups chopped

Thyme.....1 teaspoon minced

Garlic.....2 cloves minced

Fresh parsley.....1 tablespoon minced

White beans.....1 cup prepared

Parmesan cheese.....2 tablespoons

Low-fat sour cream.....1/2 cup

Freshly ground black pepper.....1 tablespoon

Directions

Preheat the oven to 350 °F (175 °C)

Mix the ingredients together in a large bowl. Transfer to a glas or ceramic dish and bake for 20 minutes.

Serve warm with whole-grain bread, crackers or vegetables fc dipping.

Nutritional analysis per serving

Serving size: Approx 1/2 cup

Total carbohydrate 14 g

Dietary fiber 6 g

Sodium 71 mg

Saturated fat 1 g

Total fat 2 g

Trans fat 0 g

Cholesterol 6 mg

Protein 5 g

Monounsaturated fat 1 g

Calories 94

Sugars 0 g

Peach Honey Spread

Peaches are full of vitamins, minerals, protein and beta carotene that help prevent cancer. The fiber content of peache assists with healthy digestion. The peach alkaline levels aid i the relief of digestive abnormalities and peaches also contai properties that bring down cholesterol levels.

This tasty spread is great with pancakes, waffles, roasted por roasted chicken and even on toast!

Serves 6

Ingredients

Fresh cranberries.....1 cup chopped

Unsweetened peach halves.....1 – 15 ounce can, drained

Honey.....2 tablespoons

Cinnamon.....1/2 teaspoon

Directions

Put the drained unsweetened peach halves in a mixer and set it t chop. When the peaches have a chunky texture comparable t applesauce, transfer them to a large bowl. Add the honey an cinnamon to the peaches. Mix with a large spoon.

Chill in the refrigerator until ready to serve or serve warm ove your favorite dish.

Nutritional analysis per serving

Serving size: 1/3 cup

Total fat 0 g

Calories 60

Protein 0.5 g

Cholesterol 0 mg

Total carbohydrate 16 g

Dietary fiber 1 g

Monounsaturated fat 0 g

Saturated fat 0 g

Sodium 4 mg

CPSIA information can be obtained
at www.ICGtesting.com
Printed in the USA
BVHW041123080221
599629BV00005B/296

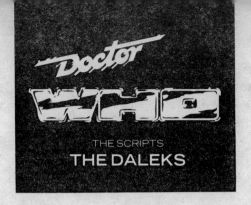

Doctor WHO

THE SCRIPTS
THE DALEKS

Other titles in the *DOCTOR WHO* scripts series:

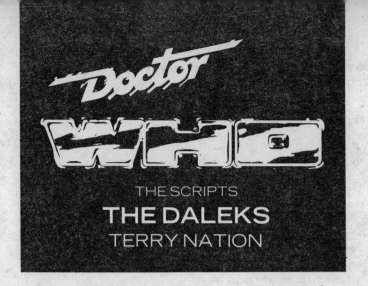

Doctor WHO

THE SCRIPTS

THE DALEKS

TERRY NATION

TITAN BOOKS

LONDON

DOCTOR WHO *THE SCRIPTS*: THE DALEKS
ISBN 1 85286 145 2

Published by
Titan Books Ltd
58 St Giles High St
London WC2H 8LH

First edition December 1989
10 9 8 7 6 5 4 3 2 1

By arrangement with BBC Books, a division of BBC Enterprises Ltd

Typeset by Photoprint, Torquay, Devon.
Printed and bound in Great Britain by Cox and Wyman Ltd, Reading,
Berkshire

CONTENTS

Every now and then there occurs a 'moment' in television history. In this respect *Doctor Who* may well be unique, for in the space of only a few weeks it produced not one but two such moments.

The first was the original episode of the series which, for people who have seen it recently still weaves its magic. The second was the appearance of those 'animated pepper pots', perhaps more widely known as the Daleks.

Within the space of seven weeks – the duration of Terry Nation's story introducing them – the Daleks had become household names, and children all over Britain were grating 'Ex-ter-min-ate' at each other in school playgrounds. So powerful was the impact of this story that the first, *The Tribe of Gum* seems – until the advent of video recordings many years later – to have been completely overshadowed; and as a result Terry Nation became credited by some as the creator not only of the Daleks but also, mistakenly, of *Doctor Who* itself. To this day, the error is repeated occasionally in the media: as well as in the British edition of the board game 'Trivial Pursuit' and even *Radio Times*.

At first sight the Daleks seemed to go directly against the edict of *Doctor Who*'s true creator, Sydney Newman, that there were to be no 'Bug-Eyed Monsters' ('BEM's). Producer Verity Lambert argued, quite reasonably, that the Daleks could not be classed as 'BEM's; they were not monsters borrowed wholesale from the B-movies. Indeed, a great deal of thought had gone into their evolution. The Daleks were the sad result of a nuclear war on a far-distant planet; as too were the handsome Thals, descendants of a warrior race. Though, as the Daleks epitomised the worst results of nuclear warfare, so the Thals were a sign of hope.

An early version of the script had the Daleks and Thals each believing the other had caused a devastating war. In the end it turned out that neither side was to blame, as a third party from Outer Space had fired the first shots. The story ended with the Thals and Daleks joining the now peaceful third party to rebuild their planet, Skaro. This was rejected by Lambert on the grounds that the overall story would have become just a little too pat and twee. Any credibility the production team might have been trying to establish would have been undermined and, in the early days of a serial, winning over the audience was – and still is – a very important objective.

As the script changed, it became a very powerful tale of adventure and morality. The Doctor's apparently inhuman disregard for the affairs of others – gradually modified later in the programme's history to become the Time-Lord's law of non-interference – first endangers the Time travellers and then effectively puts the Thal race in peril when he suggests using them to regain the TARDIS' lost fluid link. This is one of the strong moral points of the story, played out in the dialogue between the Doctor's companions, with Ian Chesterton arguing that the Thals must choose their own destiny, and Barbara Wright agreeing with the Doctor. In the end it is Ian who makes the Thals face their 'real' selves: that is, the 'selves' which viewers of the sixties would expect to see. As the years passed, the idea that Evil must be fought was to become a primary philosophy of the Doctor; not surprising, this, since just about everything 'evil' tried to kill him.

The story also suggests that we should not fear the unknown or, in the Daleks' case, the unlike. It is a shame, however, that traditional prejudices still endure; the 'good' Thals are handsome, and the 'bad' Daleks are ugly. How much more poignant if these stereotypes had been reversed, as was to happen in the later story, *'Galaxy Four'*.

In these early episodes of the series the TARDIS crew had yet to become friends, but already a certain fondness for the Doctor, and certainly for Susan, had crept in. The Doctor's occasional absent-mindedness was established, in particular by his muddling of Chesterton's name; this happened frequently enough for Ian to make a specific comment about it.

It is impossible to write about the Daleks without touching on their design. This story was one of the earliest BBC productions to take place on an alien planet, and alien it certainly was. As all the vegetation was dead, the image of the petrified plants was to be scarcely recognisable from plant-life on Earth. The flower found by Susan, though bearing a slight resemblance to an oversized crocus, had to be very fragile; the effect was achieved by making the plant from sugar, which also gave it a very fine structure.

The model of the Dalek city, originally built on a much smaller scale, lived up to the characters' description of it in Episode One. Mysterious, vast, and shrouded in mist, it presented a striking image at the foot of the mountains. The early electronic matte technique used to show the TARDIS crew looking down on the city remains impressive even in these days of 'high-tech' video effects. The technique was used again later when a Dalek fires at Ian inside the city, blistering the surface of a wall. In reality the wall was not next to Ian at all, but filmed separately and then merely superimposed; once again the effect was very convincing.

The interior of the city was deliberately kept simple, but was nevertheless very cleverly designed. Most notable was the fact that the city was built for Daleks. This may seem like stating the obvious, however. Nowadays most of the architecture in *Doctor Who* for alien cultures (including the Daleks since 1970) is designed for human actors to walk through, with little consideration for the anatomy of the aliens for whom the buildings are supposedly constructed. This was not the case when the series started and simple design principle added much to the claustrophobic feel of the early episodes of *The Daleks*, the human characters frequently having to crouch as they made their way through the Dalek city. The City's interior doors incorporated a variety of unusual features. The most common type pivoted at the base on one side, sliding up into the wall; this made it possible for Ian to stop the cell door from closing (in Episode Three) by putting something on the floor in its path. Also all the controls within the city were designed to look as if they were meant to be operated by the Daleks' sucker-sticks. By comparison, when one looks at the sets of more recent episodes, the controls, switches etc. are often relatively human in appearance.

Finally, of course, there are the Daleks themselves. Legend has it that the eventual design was inspired by a pepper-pot in a restaurant, although it is only fair to point out that their designer, Raymond Cusick vehemently denies this! In fact the final design bears only some resemblance to the description in the original script, which is very sparse in itself:

> 'Hideous machine-like creatures. They are legless, moving on a round base. They have no human features. A lens on a flexible shaft acts as an eye; arms with mechanical grips for hands. The creatures hold strange weapons in their hands.'

The design of the Daleks was a compromise of material. Raymond Cusick had wanted to build them from fibreglass, with lights flashing in the hemispheres on the Dalek 'skirt'. Misinformed that fibreglass would be too expensive, Cusick then had the Daleks built from wood.

They were not all exactly the same. One Dalek had a powerful magnet placed in its sucker to pick things up. Although not specifically intended to be visible, often it was. Another Dalek had a camera iris built into its eye-piece, used to great effect by directors Christopher Barry and Richard Martin.

These two differences were not, however, sufficient for Barry to be able to distinguish between Daleks; during rehearsals, he had numbers stuck on each one and literally directed by numbers. This explains why some rehearsal photographs from the story show Daleks with numbers crayoned on the back of their 'heads'.

The operators who had the uncomfortable task of sitting inside the hot and very cramped interiors of the machines were also partially responsible for the sheer believability of the Daleks. Not content to move the Daleks around only to cover distance, they constantly shifted from side to side and somehow gave the impression that they were hovering slightly on the spot. This is something which more recent directors – who have occasionally complained about the difficulty of shooting dynamic-looking Dalek scenes – might do well to remember.

One further aspect of the Daleks' success was the extermination effect. The negative effect was achieved very simply by flicking a switch in the production gallery during recording; phase reversing. Although the whole picture was affected, the minds of viewers focused on the unfortunate victim. In the late 1980s the technique is now very refined, and the Dalek extermination effect is confined to the victim's figure only. Whether this more modern approach is more or less effective than the original, it is left to the viewer to decide.

Finally, *The Daleks* is notable for one or two other special effects. In the early days particularly, the scripts called for techniques not used before and designers were asked to make much from limited resources. Improvisation created the creature which, in Episode Five, rises out of the swamp from a cleverly disguised inflatable rubber ring just under the water's surface.

Televisual ingenuity also extended to the use of sets. Although the script refers to the Time travellers in the control room and living quarters, there was only one set. For scenes in the 'rest room', the background hum of the TARDIS is removed. The only place where this technique falls down is in Episode One, when the crew hear a scraping outside. They walk just a few feet across to the console, during which time the TARDIS hum mysteriously appears!

It is surely a testament to the writing of Terry Nation that such budgetary restrictions are unlikely to be noticed by the viewers of this tense drama.

CAST

MAIN CAST:

The Doctor	William Hartnell
Ian Chesterton	William Russell
Susan Foreman	Carole Ann Ford
Barbara Wright	Jacqueline Hill
Alydon	John Lee
Temmosus	Alan Wheatley
Ganatus	Philip Bond
Dyoni	Virginia Wetherell
Elyon	Gerald Curtis
Antodus	Marcus Hammond
Kristas	Jonathan Crane
Dalek operators	Michael Summerton
	Robert Jewell
	Kevin Manser
	Gerald Taylor
	Peter Murphy
Dalek voices	Peter Hawkins
	David Graham

SUPPORTING CAST

Thals	Frans van Nordo
	Lesley Hill
Thal youth	Kevin Glenny

Thal, 1st young man .... Chris Browning
       2nd young man .... Steve Pokol
       1st older man .... Eric Smith
       2nd older man .... Vez Delahunt
Thal, 1st young woman ...... Katie Cashfield
       2nd young woman ..... Jeanette Rossini
Thal, older woman .... Ruth Harrison

Alydon stand-in .... Chris Browning
Double (Antodus) .... Peter Diamond

Story Code: B

Story Title(s): The Daleks
             The Mutants

(Some BBC paperwork refers to *The Mutants* as the title of the story, but in view of the later Jon Pertwee tale of the same name, *The Daleks* has become the accepted title. It should be noted that *The Dead Planet*, although sometimes used to identify this story, is in fact merely the title of the first episode, and the use of this as an overall story title only began after the *Radio Times 10th Anniversary Special* publication erroneously called all the early stories by their first episode names, rather than by their correct titles.)

Author: Terry Nation

Film sequences recorded at Ealing Studios from 28th October 1963 to 1st November 1963. (These include the Daleks using their flame-thrower, the explosion of the Dalek Ian was in, and scenes in the swamp.)

Episode One

Title .... The Dead Planet
Duration .... 24'22"

Recorded .... 15th November 1963
(or 6th December 1963)*

Transmitted .... 21st December 1963, at 17:15:55

Episode Two

Title .... The Survivors
Duration .... 24'27"
Recorded .... 22nd November 1963
Transmitted .... 28th December 1963, at 17:15:48

Episode Three

Title .... The Escape
Duration .... 25'10"
Recorded .... 29th November 1963
Transmitted .... 4th January 1964, at 17:15:06

Episode Four

Title .... The Ambush
Duration .... 24'32"
Recorded .... 6th December 1963
and 13th December 1963
Transmitted .... 11th January 1964, at 17:14:53

---

* As always, in the case of *Doctor Who*'s early days, there is a mystery, BBC transmission paperwork shows the broadcast version of Episode One was recorded in the original slot for Episode Four, indicating some sort of re-shoot of the episode. Yet the scripts show a planned recording gap between Episodes Three and Four! Paperwork for Episode Four also conflicts, giving it two recording days: 6/12/63 and 13/12/63. Indeed, the fact that Episode Four was transmitted from a film print indicates that editing which was too complicated for those early days of video-tape was needed. If the episode had indeed been recorded over two separate studio dates, then it would have to have been transferred to film for editing. (This is known to have occurred with the story *Planet of Giants*, when two episodes were joined together to make one.) Perhaps the paperwork showing Episode One as being recorded out of sequence refers to some re-takes made during the over-long recording of Episode Four. The mystery continues . . .)

Episode Five
Title .... The Expedition
Duration .... 24'31"
Recorded .... 20th December 1963
Transmitted .... 18th January 1964, at 17:15:01

Episode Six

Title .... The Ordeal
Duration .... 26'15"
Recorded .... 3rd January 1964
Transmitted .... 25th January 1964, at 17:15:09
Episode Seven

Title .... The Rescue
Duration .... 22'24"
Recorded .... 19th January 1964
Transmitted .... 1st February 1964, at 17:17:35

All recordings took place in Studio D at the BBC's Lime Grove Studios. All transmissions were off video-tape, except Episode Four which was transmitted from a film print.

PRODUCTION CREDITS

Producer	Verity Lambert
Associate Producer	Mervyn Pinfield
Script Editor	David Whitaker
Directors	Christopher Barry
	(Episodes 1,2,4,5)
	Richard Martin (Episodes 3,6,7)
Designers	Raymond Cusick
	(Episodes 1–5,7)
	Jeremy Davies (Episode 6)
Technical Operations	
Managers	Ken MacGregor (Episodes 1–4)
	Mark Lewis (Episodes 5–7)
Lighting Supervisors	John Treays (Episodes 1,5–7)
	Geoff Shaw (Episodes 2–4)
Sound Supervisors	Jack Clayton (Episodes 1–5)
	Jack Brummitt (Episodes 6,7)
Vision Mixer	Clive Doig (Episodes 1,5)
Grams Operator	Adrian Bishop-Laggett
Production Assistant	Norman Stewart
Assistant Floor Managers ...	Michael Ferguson (Episodes 1–5)
	Jeremy Hare (Episodes 6,7)
Floor Assistant	Robert Fort (Episodes 1,5)
Secretaries	Susan Pugh
	Meg Hornby
Costume Supervisor	Daphne Dare
Make-up Supervisor	Elizabeth Blattner

Film Cameraman .... Stewart Farnell
Film Editor .... Ted Walter
Title Music composed by .... Ron Grainer
Title Music realised by .... Delia Derbyshire
Incidental Music .... Tristram Carey
Visual Effects .... Shawcraft Ltd
Camera Crew .... Number One Crew

THE DEAD PLANET

1. The TARDIS Control Room (Day).

(THE DOCTOR, SUSAN, IAN *and* BARBARA *are standing round the control console.*)

THE DOCTOR: Well, I suggest before we go outside and explore, let us clean ourselves up.

SUSAN: Yes.

THE DOCTOR: Now what does the radiation read, Susan?

SUSAN: It's reading normal, Grandfather.

(*As* SUSAN *moves away from the dial, the needle begins to rise, until it is in the danger zone. A warning light starts to flash.*)

2. A Jungle Clearing.

(*The TARDIS stands in a clearing surrounded by dense jungle. The foliage is quite unlike any seen on Earth.* BARBARA *comes out of the ship, closely followed by the others.*)

BARBARA: There's been a forest fire. Everything's sort of white and ashen.

IAN: Funny mist.

THE DOCTOR: The heat must have been indescribable . . .
Look at this soil here. Look at it! It's all turned
to sand and ashes. Extraordinary!

> (BARBARA *and* SUSAN *pick up lumps of soil
> from* THE DOCTOR*'s hands.* IAN *stops and
> looks around him, bothered by something,
> but not sure what it is.*)

THE DOCTOR: How can shrubs or trees grow in soil like that?
Hm?

IAN: Something else that's strange. There's quite a
breeze blowing.

SUSAN: Well?

IAN: Well, look at the branches and things.

SUSAN: They don't seem to be moving.

BARBARA: They're not. They're absolutely still.

> (IAN *goes to the nearest bush. He takes
> hold of a branch which snaps off at the
> first touch in a cloud of dust.*)

IAN: Huh . . . like stone, look! Very brittle stone, it
. . . it crumbles when you touch it. Look!

> (*The others examine pieces of the branch.*)

THE DOCTOR: It's petrified. How fascinating – petrified jungle.
Hm, extraordinary. Yes, I must really
investigate that. Couldn't have been
heat then. And age would merely decay.

SUSAN: What could have caused it, Grandfather?

THE DOCTOR: I don't know, I don't know. But I intend to find
out.

> (*He walks away towards the edge of the
> jungle.*)

SUSAN: Well, I'm coming too.

(*She goes after* THE DOCTOR.)

BARBARA: Ian, where are we?

IAN: I don't know.

BARBARA: Why doesn't he take us back?

IAN: I'm not sure that he can.

BARBARA: What, ever?

IAN: I hate it as much as you. I'm just as afraid. But what can we do?

BARBARA: Well, we could at least stay near the Ship.

IAN: Hm. The Ship's no good without him. We'd better keep an eye on him. He seems to have a knack of getting himself into trouble.

BARBARA: You think there's any danger?

IAN: Not necessarily . . .

BARBARA: But don't be too complacent. No, you're right, I suppose . . . I just wish . . .

IAN: We'll be all right.

BARBARA: Yes. Well, I suppose we'd better make sure he doesn't fall down and break a leg. Don't you ever think he deserves something to happen to him?

IAN: Yes.

(IAN *laughs, and he and* BARBARA *exit after the others.*)

3. THE JUNGLE.

(THE DOCTOR *pauses to examine a particular tree. Suddenly* SUSAN *squeals with surprise.*)

SUSAN: Oh Grandfather, look!

(THE DOCTOR *turns to see what she has found.* SUSAN *is kneeling down by a flowering plant.*)

It's a flower. A perfect flower. It's even kept some of its colour.

(THE DOCTOR *is preoccupied with other thoughts, and barely notices.*)

THE DOCTOR: Yes. Very pretty, very pretty. Hm.

(*He turns his attention back to examining the tree.* IAN *and* BARBARA *move into view.* SUSAN *calls to* IAN.)

SUSAN: Hey, look! Look what I've found!

(IAN *bends down to look.*)

IAN: Oh, that's beautiful!

SUSAN: Isn't it? I'm going to try and pick it, and keep it all in one piece.

(BARBARA *wanders a little way away.*)

IAN: Oh be careful, it'll be very fragile.

(IAN *kneels to help* SUSAN. *Meanwhile* BARBARA, *just out of sight of the others, sees something and recoils in terror. At the same time,* IAN *and* SUSAN *are carefully lifting the flower they have picked.*)

IAN: There we are . . .

SUSAN: Beautiful! When I get it back to the ship I'm going to put it into a glass case . . .

(*Before she can finish,* BARBARA*'s terrified cry echoes through the trees.*)

BARBARA: (*OOV*) Ian! Ian!!!

(IAN *reacts quickly, and as he rises, pushes the flower roughly into* SUSAN*'s hands: It immediately disintegrates.*)

IAN: Coming. Coming!

(He runs towards the source of BARBARA's *voice.* SUSAN *looks sadly at the powdered remains of the flower in her hands, then jumps up and follows* THE DOCTOR *after* IAN. BARBARA *is standing frozen to the spot, staring downwards.* IAN *enters.)*

IAN: What is it? What's the matter?

(He breaks off as he sees what BARBARA *is staring at: a hideous and vicious-looking reptilian creature.* IAN *shields* BARBARA *from the creature, as* THE DOCTOR *and* SUSAN *arrive. Cautiously,* IAN *starts to advance on the unmoving reptile.)*

BARBARA: No!

*(*IAN *waves his hand in front of the creature. Suddenly he starts to laugh.)*

IAN: It's all right . . . like everything else in this place. Solid stone!

*(*IAN *pats the reptile's head as the others, still cautious, approach.)*

BARBARA: It's hideous!

IAN: Yes, it is. It's also significant. Nothing on Earth could look like this.

BARBARA: It looks like some sculptor's nightmare.

THE DOCTOR: Yes, it's certainly alien to anything on your planet. But you're wrong about one thing, Chesterfield. This isn't like everything else. The animal is solidified, certainly, but it is not crumbly stone. It's metal. Yes, it always was.

IAN: What – even when it was alive? Well, that's impossible.

THE DOCTOR: Why? Can't you imagine an animal unless it's flesh, blood and bone? Hm? No, I tell you this is an entirely different formation. I should say originally it was some pliable metal, held together by a magnetic field, or an inner magnetic field, rather, and it may have had the ability to attract its victims towards it, if they were of metal too.

BARBARA: We're not on Earth, then?

THE DOCTOR: No, certainly not.

IAN: Are you sure?

THE DOCTOR: Oh, certain. And you needn't look at me like that, young man. We started this journey far too hurriedly to make any calculations. You know that as well as I do. However, we're alive.

(THE DOCTOR *goes over to join* SUSAN, *who is looking off into the distance.*)

SUSAN: Hey, Grandfather, look! The jungle ends over there.

(BARBARA *sits down on a large boulder.* IAN *stands beside her.*)

IAN: Try not to be too upset.

BARBARA: I counted so much on just going back. To things I recognise and trust. But here, there's nothing to rely on . . . nothing.

IAN: Well, there's me . . . Barbara, all I ask you to do is believe, really believe, we'll go back. We will, you know.

BARBARA: I wish I was more like you. I'm afraid I'm a very unwilling adventurer.

IAN: Well, I'm not exactly revelling in it myself.

(SUSAN *runs back out of the jungle.*)

SUSAN: Grandfather's talking about fixing our position by the stars.

IAN: Good, where is he?

SUSAN: Just over there.

BARBARA: Susan?

SUSAN: Hm?

BARBARA: Don't you have anything in the Ship that records the journeys?

SUSAN: Oh yes, there's a meter fixed to a great big bank of computers. If you feed it with the right sort of information, it can take over the controls of the Ship and deliver you to any place you want to go.

BARBARA: Then why don't we know where we are?

SUSAN: Well, it's a question of the right information, you see . . . I don't say that Grandfather doesn't know how to work the Ship, but he's so forgetful. And he will go off and . . .

Well . . . he likes to work on his own.

BARBARA: So I've noticed.

(IAN _gets up and looks around._)

SUSAN: Anyway, he's only got to do some . . . computations back in the Ship, then we can move on.

BARBARA: Well, it can't be too soon for me!

(THE DOCTOR _joins them._)

THE DOCTOR: Well now, are we ready?

(SUSAN _and_ BARBARA _turn._)

BARBARA: Oh, Doctor. Have you worked out yet how all this happened?

THE DOCTOR: No, not really, not really. Whatever it was destroyed everything that was living, but er . . . The planet is dead. Totally dead.

              (*Suddenly* IAN *calls excitedly to them.*)

IAN: (*OOV*) Barbara! Doctor! Over here.

              (*They all look in the direction of* IAN's *cry, and start towards him.*)

              4. A RIDGE AT THE EDGE OF THE JUNGLE (*EVENING*).

              (IAN *is standing at the edge of the ridge. He is staring at something in the distance as the others come up behind him.*)

THE DOCTOR: What is it, Chesterton? We really must get back.

              (*He stops as he sees what* IAN *is looking at.*)

SUSAN: Oh!

THE DOCTOR: It's fascinating!

              (*Below them, in the distance, lies an incredible metallic city.* THE DOCTOR *takes a pair of binoculars that are scarcely bigger than a normal pair of spectacles out of their case, and focuses them on the city below.*)

BARBARA: A city . . . a huge city!

IAN: Well, Doctor, can you see anything? Any sign of life?

THE DOCTOR: No, no, no . . . no sign of life. No, just the buildings, magnificent buildings. I . . .

SUSAN: Oh, let me have a look.

(*Reluctantly,* THE DOCTOR *hands the glasses to* SUSAN.)

Fabulous! You have a look.

(*By now the light is fading fast.* SUSAN *hands the glasses to* BARBARA. IAN *turns to* THE DOCTOR.)

IAN: What do you think, Doctor?

THE DOCTOR: I don't know. I don't know. Whatever it was destroyed the vegetation here certainly hasn't damaged the city. But there's no sign of life. No movement, no light, no . . . I shall know more about it when I've been down there.

BARBARA: Down there? Oh, no! We're going back to the ship.

THE DOCTOR: Now don't be ridiculous. That city down there is a magnificent subject for study and I don't intend to leave here until I've thoroughly investigated it.

IAN: Well, it's too late to talk about it now, it's getting dark. We'll discuss it when we get back to the Ship.

SUSAN: Yes, whatever you decide, it's too late to get down there now.

THE DOCTOR: Yes, yes, yes, all right then. But I assure you I'm determined to study that place.

IAN: You can do what you like, as long as you don't endanger the rest of us.

THE DOCTOR: Very well, then, I shall look at it myself. Alone.

IAN: You're the only one who can operate the Ship. I'm afraid I can't let you do that, Doctor. Your glasses?

(IAN *hands* THE DOCTOR *his binoculars. They glare at each other. Then they all begin to move back to the Ship.* THE DOCTOR *takes a last look back at the city.*)

5. *THE CITY.*

(*The city spreads out below him, its many turrets and towers rising through a thick, swirling mist.*)

6. *THE JUNGLE* (*DUSK*).

(*The four travellers push their way through the jungle, back towards the Ship.*)

IAN: I think this is the way we came.

(*As they make their way back,* SUSAN *sees a flower like the one she tried to pick earlier. Delightedly, she falls to her knees and carefully picks it. By now the others are out of view. Slowly, an awareness seems to creep over her as she senses something behind her. She spins round, searching the jungle with her eyes.*)

SUSAN: Who's there?

(*A slight sound reaches her ears, and by now she is very frightened. Slowly she backs away from the source of the noise, and then stops almost paralysed with fear. From the darkness behind her, a hand reaches out to touch her shoulder. She screams and runs after the others.*)

7. *THE JUNGLE CLEARING* (*NIGHT*).

(*IAN, BARBARA and* THE DOCTOR *are about to enter the TARDIS, when* SUSAN's

scream echoes out of the darkness. IAN
turns and runs back into the jungle.)

8. *THE JUNGLE.*

(SUSAN *runs blindly, sobbing with fear.*
She crashes through the bushes, completely
lost. Suddenly a pair of arms shoot out
from the darkness and grab her. It is IAN.
SUSAN *screams.*)

IAN: All right, Susan. It's all right. You're safe now.

9. *THE TARDIS CONTROL ROOM.*

(BARBARA is staring down at the control
console, trying to see if she can make any
sense of it all. THE DOCTOR *appears at her*
side.)

BARBARA: Did Susan tell you what frightened her?

THE DOCTOR: Yes, yes, she's convinced that someone touched
her, and I tried to make her see it wasn't
possible, but I'm afraid she wouldn't listen to
me. I wonder er . . . would you have a talk with
her?

BARBARA: Yes, of course I will.

THE DOCTOR: Yes, you know sometimes I find the gulf
between Susan's age and mine makes difficult er
. . . understanding between us.

(THE DOCTOR *is slightly embarrassed at*
making this confession, but BARBARA
quickly reassures him.)

BARBARA: I'll see what I can do.

THE DOCTOR: Oh, would you? Thank you. Thank you very
much. I'm grateful.

(*For a moment, as he smiles at* BARBARA,

we catch a glimpse of THE DOCTOR'S *charm, which although it may show itself rarely, is nonetheless considerable.* BARBARA *leaves the control room to talk to* SUSAN.)

10. THE SHIP'S LIVING AREA.

(SUSAN *is sitting at a small table, busy drawing the flower that she found. She looks up as* BARBARA *enters.*)

BARBARA: Hello.

(BARBARA *sits on the table and looks down at* SUSAN.)

SUSAN: Hello.

BARBARA: What are you doing?

SUSAN: Just drawing.

BARBARA: Well, can I see?

SUSAN: It's the flower I saw in the jungle.

BARBARA: What happened out there?

SUSAN: Oh, nothing . . .

BARBARA: Well, Ian said you were terrified. Well, something must have frightened you.

SUSAN: It's not that so much. It's . . . it's just that I'm . . . I'm fed up. No one believes me.

BARBARA: Believes what?

SUSAN: Oh, I don't know. . .

BARBARA: That there was somebody out there and they touched you on the shoulder?

SUSAN: There was someone there.

BARBARA: But you didn't see who it was?

SUSAN: No.

(SUSAN *gets up and crosses behind* BAR-

BARA. SUSAN *touches* BARBARA *on the
shoulder and, as* BARBARA *turns to look,
quickly snatches her hand away again.*
BARBARA *looks at* SUSAN.)

It was like that. A light touch on the shoulder. I
couldn't have been mistaken.

BARBARA: Well, I believe you.

SUSAN: But . . . Grandfather says that . . . it's
impossible for anyone to live out there . . .

BARBARA: Oh, Susan, it isn't that he doesn't believe you.
It's just that he finds it difficult to go against his
scientific facts.

SUSAN: I know.

BARBARA: Oh look, why don't you just try and forget it, for
the moment?

SUSAN: For the moment . . .

11. THE TARDIS CONTROL ROOM.

(THE DOCTOR *is busy examining the various
machines at the back of the control room,
and is jotting down readings in a notebook.
He is muttering to himself.* IAN *is also
looking at the various knobs and switches
on the console.*)

IAN: What's this one for?

(*He points at a control, but* THE DOCTOR *is
too absorbed to hear.*)

I don't know how you make sense of any of this.

THE DOCTOR: Hm? Quite right. Quite right.

IAN: Can you find out where we are?

(*He pauses, waiting for an answer.*)

Well, Doctor?

THE DOCTOR: Hm? Oh.

IAN: I was wondering if you've . . .

THE DOCTOR: Oh, my dear boy, these eternal questions of yours. 'Do I know where we are', I suppose?

IAN: Now listen, Doctor. I don't want to argue with you. We're fellow travellers whether we like it or not. But for heaven's sake, try and see it from our point of view. You've uprooted us violently from our own lives . . .

THE DOCTOR: You pushed your way into the Ship, young man . . .

IAN: All right, all right, I admit it . . . a small part of the blame is ours . . .

THE DOCTOR: Small!

IAN: But, naturally, we're anxious. What are we going to do? Can we live here? What do we eat? There are millions of . . .

THE DOCTOR: A very good idea. I'm hungry.

(*He moves across to the other side of the control room, muttering to himself.* IAN *follows.*)

12. *THE SHIP'S LIVING AREA.*
(THE DOCTOR *and* IAN *enter.* BARBARA *is seated at a small table, clutching her head, obviously in pain.* SUSAN *is busy squeezing some drops of fluid from a small bottle into a glass of liquid.*)

THE DOCTOR: Oh, what's the matter?

BARBARA: Oh, I've suddenly got this terrible headache.

THE DOCTOR: Oh dear, dear how irksome for you!

(*He goes over to* SUSAN.)

Oh well, this stuff is very good. This should cure it. Now, not too much dear, not too much.

SUSAN: No. Oh, Grandfather, I'm sorry I was so silly just now.

(THE DOCTOR *presses some buttons on a machine just beside* SUSAN, *and it makes a beeping sound.* SUSAN *finishes mixing the medicine and hands it to* BARBARA.)

Here try this.

BARBARA: Oh . . . it's very nice.

SUSAN: Thank you.

IAN: Let's hope it does you some good.

(THE DOCTOR *is busy chewing.* SUSAN *nudges him, and suddenly he realises that* IAN *and* BARBARA *are looking at him.*)

THE DOCTOR: Oh er . . . did you want something to eat? What would you like? Hm?

BARBARA: I'd like some bacon and eggs.

IAN: All right. Bacon and eggs.

THE DOCTOR: Bacon and eggs. Yes . . . but er . . .

SUSAN: The TARDIS is fully automatic.

(IAN *looks at her, and she smiles mischievously back at him.*)

THE DOCTOR: Oh, certainly, certainly . . .

(*He consults his notebook.*)

J,6,2.

SUSAN: J . . . 6 . . . 2.

(*She adjusts various controls on the machine.*)

THE DOCTOR: L,6.

SUSAN: L . . . 6 . . .

IAN: I hope mine doesn't taste of engine grease.

THE DOCTOR: Now, now, now, now. Don't be ridiculous!

BARBARA: Shall I get some plates and things?

SUSAN: No, there's no need to.

> (*The machine beeps again, and* THE DOC-
> TOR *opens a small hatch. He removes two
> small wrapped bars, each on its own little
> tray.*)

THE DOCTOR: Here we are then.

> (He hands one to BARBARA *and* SUSAN
> *hands the other one to* IAN.)

SUSAN: Eggs and bacon.

(IAN *and* SUSAN *stare at the bars and then look at each other.*)

BARBARA: Thank you.

THE DOCTOR: Bacon and eggs.

IAN: What, this?

SUSAN: Go on . . . try it.

> (IAN *unwraps his and picks up what looks
> like a chocolate bar. He takes a tentative
> bite.*)

THE DOCTOR: Well?

IAN: Hm, not bad. What do you think, Barbara?

> (BARBARA *tastes hers.*)

BARBARA: I think it's delicious!

IAN: My bacon's a bit salty.

THE DOCTOR: Well, it shouldn't be, it's English.

> (BARBARA *looks at* IAN *and laughs.*)

IAN: No, seriously, Doctor, this is remarkable. I
mean one bite and I taste bacon, another and I
taste the egg. How do you do it?

THE DOCTOR: Why, food has component parts, dear boy.
Flavours are rather like primary colours. You
know, you blend two to achieve a third, and so
on, etc. etc.

IAN: Well, I think it's wonderful.

(*He continues to eat as* SUSAN *turns to*
BARBARA.)

SUSAN: How's your headache now?

BARBARA: Oh, it's much better. I don't usually get them at
all.

THE DOCTOR: Susan, would you like something to eat?

SUSAN: No thanks, I'm not hungry.

THE DOCTOR: Oh child, that's unusual. I do hope your
experience outside the Ship hasn't affected you
too much?

SUSAN: No . . . I think I'll go to bed now, anyway.

THE DOCTOR: Right.

SUSAN: Do you want to know where you can sleep, Miss
Wright?

BARBARA: Oh, yes.

(*They start to leave. Suddenly they all
freeze as they hear a knocking sound from
outside the Ship.*)

IAN: Sssh! What's that?

(*There is a moment's pause. A scraping
noise is heard, again outside the Ship.
Then the knocking sounds again.*)

THE DOCTOR: The scanner!

(*He hurries over to the control console.*
IAN *and* BARBARA *quickly follow.*)

SUSAN: There was somebody there!

13. *The TARDIS Control Room.*

(THE DOCTOR *operates the scanner switch, and they all gaze up at the screen.*)

IAN: (*OOV*) Nothing. Not a thing.

SUSAN: (*OOV*) But something must have made that noise . . .

BARBARA: Look, I've had enough of this. Please can't we get out of here?

THE DOCTOR: Ah, but the city . . . I must see the city.

BARBARA: But why?

THE DOCTOR: I will not be questioned.

(*He mutters to himself.*)

Uninvited passengers. I didn't invite them into the Ship. I shall do what I want to do.

(IAN *advances on* THE DOCTOR.)

IAN: Why endanger the rest of us by staying here?

SUSAN: Grandfather! Please . . . please . . .

(*For a moment,* THE DOCTOR *looks as though he is going to argue. Then he nods and turns back to the control panel. The others relax, believing that they have won.* THE DOCTOR *starts to operate certain controls. He gives a brief backward glance at the others, and seeing that their attention is again on the scanner, he bends down and removes something from behind a panel at the base of the console. He quickly stands up again, and throws a final switch. The whine of the motors begins to build.*)

BARBARA: You know, stone trees are all very well . . . the next forest I walk through, I want them all to be made of . . .

(BARBARA's *final words are lost, as a sudden loud booming noise echoes through the Ship. The whine of the Ship's engines falters and grinds down to nothing. They immediately turn to* THE DOCTOR.)

SUSAN: What's the matter?

THE DOCTOR: I don't know. The power take-up was rising normally, and . . .

(*He throws a switch. The power hum starts to build and then falters again.*)

IAN: What's wrong?

THE DOCTOR: Oh, don't distract me, please!

SUSAN: Shall I trace it on the fault locator, Grandfather?

THE DOCTOR: Yes, I think you'd better, child.

(SUSAN *goes over to a machine at the back of the room, and starts to read from it.*)

SUSAN: K, 7.

THE DOCTOR: K 7. Ah yes, of course, the fluid link. Yes, yes, yes . . . yes . . .

(*He reaches down beneath the console and withdraws a small transparent component.*)

Yes, here we are, you see! The end of it's unscrewed itself, and the fluid has run out.

IAN: Well, have you got a spare?

THE DOCTOR: Oh no, no need for that. This is easily repaired. All we have to do is refill it.

IAN: What liquid do you need?

THE DOCTOR: Mercury.

IAN: Mercury, ah! Can I get it for you?

THE DOCTOR: No, I'm afraid you can't. We haven't any . . . at all.

IAN:	What?
THE DOCTOR:	No.
IAN:	Don't you carry a supply?
THE DOCTOR:	No, it hasn't been necessary. This hasn't happened before.
IAN:	But you must have some somewhere, surely?
THE DOCTOR:	No, no, we shall have to get some from outside.
BARBARA:	But where? There isn't anything outside but the . . .
IAN:	Yes, there's the city.
THE DOCTOR:	Yes, the city, of course, of course. We're bound to get some mercury there. Yes we're bound to. Well, I mean, what else can we do?
IAN:	It seems we have no alternative. We have to go to the city.
THE DOCTOR:	Yes, indeed. At er . . . first light, then?

(*He turns away from the others and smiles victoriously. He tosses the fluid link in his hand, and slips it into one of his pockets.*)

14. *THE TARDIS CONTROL ROOM (DAY).*

(*The travellers gaze at the scanner screen.*)

IAN:	Well, it's light enough, and there doesn't seem to be anything out there. We might as well get started. Oh, and Doctor, remember, we're going to this city to find mercury, and once we find it, we're coming straight back here. Is that clear?
THE DOCTOR:	Oh, quite so, quite so.

(*He moves towards the door.*)

15. *THE JUNGLE CLEARING.*

(THE DOCTOR *steps cautiously out of the TARDIS. The others follow.*)

IAN:	Well, shall I lead?
THE DOCTOR:	Yes, by all means.
IAN:	Oh, look!

(*They all turn to see* IAN *pointing at a small metallic box near the Ship. He moves to examine it.*)

BARBARA:	Oh, don't touch it. It might go off!
SUSAN:	Be careful!

(IAN *hesitates for a moment, but then cautiously approaches the box.*)

THE DOCTOR:	What is it, Chesterton?
IAN:	I don't know. Stand back, all of you.

(IAN *breaks off a branch from one of the petrified trees and gently prods the box. Nothing happens. He carefully picks up the box and opens it.*)

I think it's all right. A metal box . . . ha!

(*He has opened it and sees the contents.*)

It's a box of glass phials, look!

THE DOCTOR:	Hm. Let me see.
SUSAN:	Then there *was* somebody here last night. They must have dropped them. I knew I was right.
IAN:	Yes . . . sorry, Susan.

(THE DOCTOR *takes the box from* IAN.)

THE DOCTOR:	Yes, I'd like to run a few tests on those. Susan, will you take these into the Ship, please?
SUSAN:	Yes.

(*She does as she is asked.*)

THE DOCTOR: Thank you. Oh, and by the way, did you remember the food supplies?

SUSAN: Yes. A day's supply for four. That's enough, isn't it?

THE DOCTOR: Yes, ample, ample.

IAN: I trust we won't be more than a couple of hours.

THE DOCTOR: Hm!

(THE DOCTOR *glances at* IAN. SUSAN *returns, and the four of them prepare to move off.*)

IAN: Are you ready, Susan?

SUSAN: Yes!

IAN: Come on, then, off we go.

16. *THE EDGE OF THE CITY.*

(*There are no steps anywhere, only ramps. The flooring is metallic. The principal building has an impressive main entrance with doors leading off. The travellers arrive at this building and look about themselves in awe. As they draw closer,* THE DOCTOR *is holding on to* SUSAN *for support.*)

THE DOCTOR: Oh, do you mind if I sit down for a minute? I feel a bit exhausted.

IAN: Are you all right?

THE DOCTOR: Oh, yes, I'm er . . . just a bit tired. It was a long journey, and my legs are rather weak.

BARBARA: Look, why don't you rest here? Ian and I will look round and see if we . . .

THE DOCTOR: No, no, no, no, I want to look around too. I shall be all right.

IAN: I must say I don't feel too good myself . . . Look, why don't we get this over with quickly? Look for instruments, gauges, anything like that. Ideally, what we want is a laboratory.

(BARBARA *has been examining an arched*

*panel. As she passes her hand across a
small box nearby, it suddenly swings open
to reveal a passageway beyond.*)

BARBARA: Ian, look!

IAN: Why don't we separate and go different ways,
and meet back here in, say, ten minutes – right?

BARBARA: Fine, I'll go this way.

(*She sets off into the passageway.*)

THE DOCTOR: Lend me your arm would you, Susan? Thank
you.

(THE DOCTOR *and* SUSAN *move off.* IAN *is
standing by another door. Suddenly it,
too, begins to open.*)

17. *A CORRIDOR.*

(BARBARA *moves down the corridor. It is
quite narrow. As she passes, a camera lens
placed high up on the wall moves to follow
her.*)

18. *THE EDGE OF THE CITY.*

SUSAN: Let's try this one.

(SUSAN *and* THE DOCTOR *approach another
doorway.* SUSAN *waves her hand across
the opening control and the door swings
open.*)

SUSAN: There we are!

19. *INTERIOR CORRIDOR (DAY).*

(BARBARA *walks along the corridor paus-
ing occasionally to examine the walls,
unaware that a shutter has silently slid
across the corridor behind her, blocking
her retreat. As she progresses, more shut-
ters close after her.* BARBARA *reaches a*

*junction in the passageway, and turning
the corner realises that she has reached a
dead end. She shrugs and turns to go back
the way she has come, but suddenly
realises that it is now closed. She begins to
panic, and beats against the wall with her
fist. She looks for a crack or an opening,
but is unable to find one. She turns and
runs down the one remaining corridor.)*

20. *EXTERIOR EDGE OF THE CITY (DAY).*

(THE DOCTOR *and* SUSAN *return.* IAN *is
already waiting for them.*)

IAN:	Ah, there you are! Any luck?
SUSAN:	No, how about you?
IAN:	No . . . no luck . . . Barbara should be here by now.

(He calls to her.)

Barbara? Barbara?

(There is no reply.)

We'll give her a couple of minutes more. Then if
she's not back, we'll have to go and look for her.

21. *A CORRIDOR.*

(BARBARA'S *footsteps echo as she runs
down the corridor. Again she reaches a
dead end. Sobbing slightly, she turns back
again. As she turns, she finds her way
blocked by yet another panel. In frustration she pounds on the panel and, exhaust-
ing herself, makes an effort to control her
tears. She puts her cheek against the cool
wall and then, pulling herself together,*

turns to retreat the way she has come. Her face fills with horror. She is now trapped in an area not more than a few feet across. Without warning the whole room begins to descend.)

22. THE EDGE OF THE CITY.

IAN: We've waited long enough for her. We must go and find her.

(THE DOCTOR and SUSAN move to follow IAN. They enter the door that BARBARA went through and vanish from sight.)

23. A CORRIDOR (DAY).

(BARBARA advances, slowly, towards a junction. Behind her, unseen, a panel slides open with a slight noise and a mechanical arm emerges. She hears the noise and turns round in time to see the thing that is advancing towards her.)

Next Episode:
THE SURVIVORS

EPISODE TWO

THE SURVIVORS

1. *A Corridor (Day).*

(BARBARA *advances, slowly, towards a junction. Behind her, unseen, a panel slides open with a slight noise and a mechanical arm emerges. She hears the noise and turns round in time to see the thing that is advancing towards her.*)

2. *The Reception Hall.*

(IAN *waves his hand over the door control and it swings open.* IAN *and* THE DOCTOR, *supported by* SUSAN, *enter the doorway and look around. They are in a hall with a number of passageways and doors that lead off it.*

IAN: Barbara . . . Barbara!

(*As he speaks,* IAN's *voice echoes around the hallway.* THE DOCTOR *and* SUSAN *move to the other side of the hall, while* IAN *looks into a doorway leading off.*)

Barbara!

(SUSAN *touches another door control, and the door opens.*)

SUSAN: Miss Wright?

(IAN *meanwhile has opened a third door, and peers through it.*)

IAN: Barbara?

SUSAN: Hey, there's a corridor over here!

(IAN *moves over to join them.*)

IAN: We might as well see where it goes to. Come on!

(THE DOCTOR, *however, has caught a faint sound and strains to hear more.*)

THE DOCTOR: Wait!

IAN: What's the matter?

THE DOCTOR: Listen!

(*Far away, there is a vague, irregular ticking sound.*)

SUSAN: I can hear it. A ticking noise.

THE DOCTOR: Quiet, child, listen!

IAN: Yes . . . over here somewhere.

(*They all cross the hall.*)

THE DOCTOR: It's stopped now.

(*They halt and listen. The ticking starts again.*)

SUSAN: Hey, there it is again!

IAN: It's coming from in here.

(IAN *leads the way to yet another door. They stop outside and listen. The ticking is louder.*)

3. THE INSTRUMENT ROOM.

(*The door opens and* IAN *appears. Large instruments stand on the floor.* THE DOCTOR *and* SUSAN *follow* IAN *into the room. Unnoticed, the door closes silently behind them.*)

IAN: Ah, this is more hopeful! We ought to find some mercury here.

THE DOCTOR: Hm. Measuring equipment. But measuring what?

(IAN *comes over to see the machine which* THE DOCTOR *is examining.*)

Look here, look at this drum! The ink's still quite wet.

(THE DOCTOR *moves his finger over the line on the drum – it smudges.*)

IAN: Yes . . . I'm trying to imagine what sort of people these are.

THE DOCTOR: They're intelligent, anyway, very intelligent.

IAN: Yes, but how do they use their intelligence? What form does it take?

THE DOCTOR: Oh, as if that matters! What these instruments tell us is that we're in the midst of a . . . a very, very advanced, civilized society.

SUSAN: Here it is, the thing that's ticking . . . it's over here! It's a geiger counter.

(*The machine's needle is flickering back and forth, firmly in the zone marked 'danger'.*)

IAN: But look at the needle . . . it's past the danger point!

THE DOCTOR: Yes, yes, that explains a lot of things, doesn't it? The jungle turned to stone . . . The barren soil and the fact that we're not feeling well.

IAN: Radiation sickness?

THE DOCTOR: Yes, I'm afraid so. The atmosphere here is polluted with a very high level of fall-out, and we've been walking around in it completely unprotected.

IAN: What? Then how do you explain the buildings – they're intact?

THE DOCTOR: A neutron bomb. Yes . . . it destroys all human tissues, but leaves the building and machinery intact. Mmm, yes.

IAN: What? But how much radiation? How badly?

THE DOCTOR: Oh . . . we need . . . we need drugs . . . to be treated.

IAN: But where are we going to find them?

SUSAN: The TARDIS'll have to take us to another time and place where we can be cured.

IAN: But don't you remember, we can't move the Ship until we find the mercury for the fluid link?

(THE DOCTOR *looks distinctly uncomfortable.*)

THE DOCTOR: For the fluid link, yes. Yes, I'm afraid I cheated a little on that. I was determined to see the city, but everybody wanted to go on and, well . . . to avoid arguments . . . in short . . . there's er . . . nothing wrong with the fluid link.

(*He holds it out for* IAN *to see.* IAN *takes it.*)

SUSAN: What! Grandfather, do you mean to say that you risked leaving the Ship . . . just to see this place?

IAN: You fool! You old fool!

THE DOCTOR: Abuse me as much as you like, Chesterton. The point is . . . we need an immediate return to the Ship, and I suggest we leave at once.

IAN: We're not leaving until we've found Barbara!

THE DOCTOR: Very well, you may stay and search for her if you wish, but Susan and I are going back to the Ship. Now, come along, child.

IAN: All right, carry on, fine . . . How far do you think you'll get . . . without this?

> (*He holds up the fluid link. For the first time* THE DOCTOR *shows some concern. He advances on* IAN.)

THE DOCTOR: Now give that to me.

IAN: Not until we've found Barbara.

THE DOCTOR: Give it to me, I say!

> (*He snatches at the fluid link, but* IAN *easily avoids him.*)

IAN: No! It's time you faced up to your responsibilities. You got us here, now I'm going to make sure that you get us back.

THE DOCTOR: Chesterton, this is . . .

IAN: We're wasting time. We should be looking for Barbara.

> (THE DOCTOR *fumes in silence.*)

SUSAN: He's right, Grandfather. We are wasting time.

THE DOCTOR: Oh, child! If only you'd think as an adult sometimes . . .

> (*He holds his head, realising the futility of arguing further.*)

Oh, very well, very well. Let's go, then, let's go.

(IAN *puts the fluid link into his pocket. They move towards the door.*)

4. *THE RECEPTION ROOM.*

(THE DOCTOR, SUSAN *and* IAN *enter, then stop dead in their tracks at what they see.* SUSAN *screams and* THE DOCTOR *clutches her protectively. Standing before them are a number of identical machine-like creatures. Each has a domed head, with what resembles a kind of eye-piece sticking out on the end of a stalk at the front. Beneath the dome are a pair of mechanical rods. One has a sucker on its end, the other is shorter and of unknown purpose. The bottom half of each creature consists of a roughly circular skirt-like façade, made up of a number of panels, each with a series of small domes on it. This widens as it goes downwards, ending in a band that forms the base of each creature. The creatures glide across the floor without any visible sign of propulsion and surround* THE DOCTOR, SUSAN *and* IAN. *Without warning, one of them addresses the travellers in a harsh electronic tone.*)

DALEK: You will move a-head of us and fol-low my di-rec-tions. This way.

(*The Dalek glides towards a doorway. The travellers do not move.*)

Im-med-iat-ely!

(*Reluctantly* THE DOCTOR *and* SUSAN *start to follow.* IAN *glances around him, weighing up the chances of escape. He does not move.*)

I said im-med-iat-ely!

(IAN *breaks away and makes a dash for the corridor.*)

DALEK: Fire!

(*Immediately several of the Daleks fire at* IAN, *using the shorter of their two 'arms' which is obviously some sort of electric gun. He screams in agony and crumples to the floor.*)

IAN: My legs . . . my legs . . .

(SUSAN *moves to help him but the Dalek stops her.* THE DOCTOR *grabs hold of her before she incurs their further wrath.*)

DALEK: Stop!

(*The Dalek glides across to* IAN, *who is trying futilely to stand up.*)

Your legs are par-a-lysed. You will re-cov-er short-ly, un-less you force us to use our wea-pons a-gain. In that case, the con-dit-ion will be per-man-ent.

(*The Dalek turns his eye-stick towards* SUSAN *and* THE DOCTOR.)

You two. Help him.

IAN: My legs . . . my legs . . . I can't use my legs.

5. A CELL.

(BARBARA *sits in the corner of a featureless room, her head in her hands. She looks up at a sound from outside.*)

DALEK: (*OOV*) Here.

(BARBARA *gets to her feet as the door slides open. In the corridor outside* SUSAN *and* THE DOCTOR *are supporting* IAN. *A Dalek is behind them. They enter the cell and* BARBARA *rushes delightedly towards them.*)

BARBARA: Susan! Ian!

SUSAN: Miss Wright!

IAN: Oh, Barbara! Thank heaven we've found you. Are you all right?

BARBARA: Yes.

(*She realises suddenly that* IAN *is injured.*)

What's the matter? What happened?

IAN: Oh, I'm all right.

SUSAN: He tried to get away and they hurt him.

(*The door slides shut, leaving them alone in the cell.*)

BARBARA: Well, can't you stand up?

IAN: Not without help. The feeling's coming back, don't worry.

BARBARA: Come over here.

(THE DOCTOR *and* SUSAN *lower* IAN *to the floor, with his back propped up against the wall.* THE DOCTOR, *by now looking extremely ill, sits down in a corner.* SUSAN *and* BARBARA *stay with* IAN.)

IAN: How about you, Barbara? We tried to look for you, then those machines caught us.

BARBARA: Well, they trapped me in some sort of lift . . . It seemed to go down for ages.

IAN: They didn't hurt you?

BARBARA:	No . . . Ian . . . What are they?
IAN:	I don't know, Barbara, did you notice anything? I mean when they were moving you about? Any little thing may help us.
BARBARA:	No, nothing much. They moved me from floor to floor, always in lifts. Where we are now must be miles underground. Oh, there wasn't any furniture now, come to think about it.
IAN:	I'm afraid that's not very much help.
BARBARA:	Ian, do you think they really are . . . just machines?
IAN:	What do you mean?
BARBARA:	Well, I was going to say . . . do you think there's someone inside them?

(SUSAN *laughs nervously.*)

IAN:	It's a point . . . we haven't any idea what's inside them.
BARBARA:	I tried to think of how I could get away from them. But then I began to feel so weak and giddy. It's getting worse now. I think they must have drugged me in some way.
IAN:	It's not that. Barbara, we've got radiation sickness, all of us. The Doctor's pretty badly hit.
BARBARA:	Well, how do you know it's radiation?
SUSAN:	We found a geiger counter. It seems that all the time we've been in the open we've been exposed to it.
BARBARA:	Well, what's going to happen to us?

(THE DOCTOR *is propped up against the wall, his eyes closed.*)

THE DOCTOR:	Unless . . . unless we get treatment . . . we shall die.

(*His voice fades to a whisper.*)

Yes . . . we shall die . . .

6. *THE DALEK CONTROL ROOM.*

(*Two Daleks are watching their prisoners on a round viewing screen set into a wall.*)

DALEK TWO: Bring in the old man Thal pri-son-er.

(*The other Dalek appears to be reading from one of the instruments in front of them.*)

DALEK ONE: Two hun-dred days a-go, the ra-dia-tion count was nine-ty-three.

DALEK TWO: It is now fif-ty-eight. An im-press-ive re-duc-tion.

DALEK ONE: It is still e-nough to des-troy. Our pri-son-ers are show-ing pre-lim-in-ary sta-ges of sick-ness al-ready.

DALEK TWO: We know the Thals are a-ble to live on the sur-face.

DALEK ONE: And then they must have found im-mun-ity.

DALEK TWO: Per-haps it is a drug. Is it fail-ing them now? Why are these four show-ing signs of ra-diat-ion sick-ness?

DALEK ONE: A few que-stions will re-duce the my-ste-ry.

(*The door opens and* THE DOCTOR *enters, followed by another Dalek. He is very weak now, but summons all his energy. The Dalek urges him into a pool of light.*)

Do not move out of the light. Sit on the floor.

(THE DOCTOR *sinks to the floor.*)

DALEK TWO: You are one of the Thal Peo-ple?

THE DOCTOR: I don't understand you.

DALEK ONE: Why are you suf-fer-ing from ra-diat-ion?

THE DOCTOR: Why? Because we were not aware of it until it was too late, that's why.

DALEK TWO: No, that is not true. We know the Thals have ex-ist-ed out-side our city.

DALEK ONE: The truth is, your sup-ply of drugs has failed and you came in-to the city to see if you could find more.

THE DOCTOR: No, no. Thals? What's he talking about? We're not Thals, or whatever you may call them. Can't you see we're very ill?

DALEK TWO: You and your com-pan-ions need a drug to stay a-live.

THE DOCTOR: We have no drugs.

(*Suddenly realisation dawns.*)

A drug? A drug . . . The drugs left outside the TARDIS.

(*He struggles to his feet.*)

DALEK TWO: 'Tar-dis'? He is be-com-ing de-lir-ious. I do not un-der-stand his words.

(THE DOCTOR *rises.*)

THE DOCTOR: Listen to me . . .

DALEK ONE: Stay in the light!

THE DOCTOR: My friends and I are travellers. We did find something in the forest, near our . . . our encampment. They may be the drugs you're referring to. Why not let one of us go and bring the phials here . . . under guard, if necessary?

DALEK TWO: We can-not move out-side the city.

THE DOCTOR: Very well, then, let one of us go, and hold the others until he returns.

DALEK ONE:	Pro-vid-ing who-ever you send un-der-stands the rest of you will be held re-spons-ible for his re-turn.
THE DOCTOR:	He will have our lives in his hands. That is enough.
DALEK ONE:	Then we a-gree.

(THE DOCTOR *weakly sinks to his knees.*)

THE DOCTOR:	Tell me something about the people, the Thals. Mmm?
DALEK TWO:	Ov-er five hun-dred years a-go there were two ra-ces on this pla-net. We, the Da-leks, and the Thals. Af-ter the Neu-tronic war, our Da-lek fore-fath-ers re-tired in-to the city, pro-tect-ed by our ma-chines.
THE DOCTOR:	And the Thals?
DALEK ONE:	Most of them pe-rished in the war, but we know that there are sur-viv-ors. They must be dis-gust-ing-ly mu-tat-ed, but the fact that they have sur-vived tells us they must have a drug that pre-serves the life force.
THE DOCTOR:	And knowing that these mutated creatures exist outside the city, you're willing to send one of us in amongst them?
DALEK ONE:	As you say your-self, all your lives de-pend on it.

7. THE CELL (EVENING).

(SUSAN *and* BARBARA *are helping* IAN *to regain the use of his legs. They are supporting him as he tries to walk.*)

BARBARA:	Is it any easier?
IAN:	Yes, I think it is. I'm going to try and stand on my own.
SUSAN:	Be careful!
IAN:	I'll be all right. Huh . . . that's not too bad.

(*He takes a step or two, obviously still in great pain.*)

BARBARA: Why don't you sit down for a minute?

IAN: No, no, no, I'll be all right. I . . .

(*He tries again, but falls.*)

IAN: Oh, it's no good!

BARBARA: Come on, sit down. It'll wear off in time.

(BARBARA *sits beside* IAN, *clutching her head.*)

IAN: How are you feeling, Barbara?

BARBARA: Oh . . . not too good.

IAN: Susan?

SUSAN: Well, it doesn't seem to have affected me as much as the rest of you.

(*The door to the cell slides open and* THE DOCTOR *staggers in.*)

SUSAN: Grandfather!

IAN: Are you all right?

(BARBARA *and* SUSAN *help him to sit down.*)

SUSAN: What happened?

(THE DOCTOR *is getting steadily weaker, and is finding even speech difficult.*)

THE DOCTOR: In a moment, child . . . the phial of drugs left outside the TARDIS, remember?

BARBARA: Yes, what about them?

THE DOCTOR: It's possible that they may have been anti-radiation gloves . . . drugs . . .

(THE DOCTOR *is becoming delirious.*)

I . . . I can't be certain, but it does give us a chance. The people here, whoever they may be, are very eager to get hold of them.

IAN: Well, none of us are in very good shape to go and get them.

BARBARA: Well, I could do it . . .

IAN: No, it must be me.

BARBARA: But you can't walk!

IAN: Oh, I'll be all right in a couple of hours.

THE DOCTOR: Whoever goes must be very careful. As far as I can ascertain, the creatures out there are the ones who dropped the box. They're called Thals . . . they're mutations.

IAN: So it wasn't our captors who left the drugs behind?

THE DOCTOR: No . . . if they _were_ drugs. I've learned quite a lot from the Daleks.

IAN: The who?

THE DOCTOR: The Daleks – our captors here. Oh, if I didn't feel so . . . But I was right about a neutron bomb. The Daleks built this underground city as a kind of huge shelter.

IAN: But what about the . . . the . . . What did you call them? The Thals?

(_By now,_ THE DOCTOR _is barely conscious._)

THE DOCTOR: I . . .

IAN: I mean, how did they survive out there? Doctor? Doctor! I must get that drug quickly.

(SUSAN _feels_ THE DOCTOR'_s forehead._)

SUSAN: He's burning hot.

IAN: Yes. As soon as they take me to the surface, I'll ask for water. In the meantime you must keep him as cool as you possibly can. I think there's some life coming back into my toes.

(SUSAN *rubs them for him.*)

SUSAN: You can't go alone, Ian. I'll have to go with you.

IAN: No, I want you to stay here, Susan.

SUSAN: But I can't. I must go with you.

IAN: Oh, don't argue with me!

SUSAN: You can't get into the Ship.

IAN: Oh, all right then, give me the key.

SUSAN: It's not just a question of turning the key – the whole lock comes away from the door.

IAN: Susan . . . supposing these Daleks insist that only one of us goes. Then I'll have to take the key, and I'll have to go on trying until the door opens.

SUSAN: No, you'll jam the lock. Look, it's a defence mechanism. There are twenty-one different holes inside the lock. There's one right place and twenty wrong ones. If you make a mistake you'll, well . . . the whole inside of the lock will melt.

IAN: There's nothing else for it, then. We must go together.

(SUSAN *nods.*)

IAN: Come on, then. Let's see if I can walk.

(BARBARA *tries weakly to get up.*)

No, it's all right, Barbara. You take it easy, rest. My right leg is better, you know.

(*He falls over again.*)

I've got feeling in this one. But the left is just pins and needles.

(*The door slides open again and a Dalek appears.*)

DALEK:	You must leave now.

(IAN *starts to rise, painfully*.)

IAN:	I'm not well enough yet.
DALEK:	You must leave now.
IAN:	My legs!
DALEK:	Which one of you is go-ing?

(IAN *tries to struggle to his feet; but it is useless and he falls again, despair etched on his face.*)

IAN:	You must give me more time.
SUSAN:	Can't you see how weak he is?
DALEK:	There are oth-ers.

(BARBARA *tries to stand, but she falls back weakly against the wall.*)

BARBARA:	Oh, Ian, I can't . . . the whole room's going round. Oh!

(SUSAN *realises that she is the only one capable of the journey. She is horrified at the thought of travelling through the jungle on her own and looks round helplessly at* IAN.)

SUSAN:	Must I? Alone?
BARBARA:	You can't let her go alone. She's just a child. Plead with them . . . anything . . .
IAN:	Susan, you see how ill they both are. We can't afford to wait until I can walk. An hour might make all the difference.
SUSAN:	I'm so afraid!
IAN:	Go on . . .

(IAN *smiles at her, trying to give her courage.*)

Don't stop for anything. Straight there, straight back!

DALEK: Are you re-ady?

IAN: Yes, all right.

SUSAN: I'm coming now.

(*As she goes out, she turns to look at the others, but is roughly pushed out by the Dalek.*)

BARBARA: Ian . . . the others . . . in the forest. He said they were mutations . . .

IAN: But what else could I do?

(*He pounds his still-numb leg in frustration.*)

8. *THE DALEK CONTROL ROOM* (*NIGHT*).

(*Several Daleks are clustered round the various control panels. Another Dalek glides into the room.*)

DALEK ONE: The child has set out.

DALEK TWO: Her di-rect-ion is be-ing fol-lowed on the ranger-scopes?

DALEK ONE: Yes.

DALEK TWO: Mark her move-ments care-ful-ly. If there are more Thal peo-ple li-ving in the jun-gle she will try to con-tact them.

DALEK ONE: I un-der-stand. If she re-turns with the drug, am I to al-low the pri-son-ers to use it?

DALEK TWO: No. They will die in time. Their on-ly va-lue is in bring-ing us en-ough of the Thal drug to dup-lic-ate it for our own use.

DALEKS ONE
AND TWO: Yes . . . At last we have a chance . . .

9. *THE CELL.*

(THE DOCTOR *is still sitting in a corner, his eyes closed.* BARBARA *and* IAN *are looking at him with concern.*)

BARBARA: He's getting worse!

IAN: How long did the Doctor say we could last without treatment? Forty-eight hours?

BARBARA: I don't know. It's hit him so badly, Ian.

IAN: Yes. How are you feeling?

BARBARA: Oh, I . . . I ache all over. I have difficulty in keeping my eyes open.

IAN: Yes, I'm about the same.

(*He glares at* THE DOCTOR.)

All his fault! Had to have his own way . . . see the city.

BARBARA: Oh, Ian, that doesn't help!

IAN: Oh, I know, I know.

BARBARA: We must wait. That's all we can do.

IAN: Wait, yes. An hour ago I thought we might try and escape . . . watch their movements, make a plan . . . There's always a chance. Now we're too late. I think even if they left the doors wide open, we wouldn't have the strength to crawl through them.

BARBARA: How long has she been gone?

IAN: About an hour . . . she should just be on the edge of the jungle by now.

10. *THE JUNGLE.*

(*There is a flash of lightning and a loud rumble of thunder.* SUSAN *is hurrying through the jungle. As the lightning flashes, we see brief glimpses of undefined figures moving in the trees. She runs faster and faster through the jungle, her panic rapidly getting the better of her. Suddenly she trips, and lies there stunned for a moment. She looks up and gasps in terror at what she sees.*)

11. THE CELL.

(THE DOCTOR *is lying flat out on a bench.* IAN *and* BARBARA *are attending to him.*)

BARBARA: He's so hot. It's . . . it's like a fever.

IAN: Yes, his breathing's so bad. What do you think, Barbara?

BARBARA: I don't know. Even if Susan got back now . . . I don't know whether she'd be in time. Give . . . give me his coat.

IAN: Here you are.

(IAN *hands her* THE DOCTOR's *jacket. She rolls it up and puts it under his head. She stands up, but staggers.* IAN *reaches out to steady her.*)

IAN: Barbara, come on now!

BARBARA: No, I'm . . . I'm all right.

IAN: No, you sit down.

(*He helps her to sit down and feels her brow.*)

IAN: No, you rest, you can't do anything more for him.

BARBARA: It's so hot in here.

IAN: Yes, now you try and sleep, Barbara. Try and sleep.

BARBARA: Yes . . . I'd like to sleep . . . It's so hot . . .

(BARBARA *closes her eyes.* IAN *makes her as comfortable as possible, and realises he can now walk. He moves towards the door, but suddenly doubles up in pain from the radiation sickness.*)

IAN: Hurry, Susan . . . hurry, Susan!

12. *THE JUNGLE.*

(SUSAN *is on her knees. She scrabbles backwards away from the thing she can see in the shadows. She claws at the ground and, with a movement born of desperation flings a handful of ash up towards the shadow. Then in an instant she is on her feet, running away as fast as she can.*)

13. *THE DALEK CONTROL ROOM.*

(*Four Daleks are standing by the control panel.*)

DALEK ONE: I have just come from the pri-son-ers. The old man is dy-ing.

DALEK TWO: Then he must die. There is no help we can give him. How are the oth-ers?

DALEK ONE: The wo-man is sleep-ing ve-ry heav-i-ly. The young man fights ag-ainst it.

DALEK TWO: What of the girl? Has she reached the jungle?

DALEK ONE: Yes. The ran-ger-scopes tracked her that far. Now they have lost her.

14. *THE JUNGLE CLEARING.*

(*Lightning flashes again to reveal the familiar shape of the TARDIS.* SUSAN *breaks through into the clearing and gazes with evident relief at the Ship. She listens*

*for sounds of pursuit, but there are none.
She runs quickly across and puts her key
in the lock of the Ship. She glances behind
her briefly, then enters.)*

15. *THE TARDIS CONTROL ROOM.*

(With a tremendous sense of relief, SUSAN
*enters. She goes straight over to the
console and operates the control to close
the doors. Then she goes over to the chair
where the drugs were left and, picking
them up, clasps them gratefully. Suddenly
she remembers* IAN's *parting words to
her . . .)*

IAN: (*OOV*) Don't stop for anything . . . Straight
there, straight back! An hour might make all the
difference.

SUSAN: I must . . . I must.

*(She operates the door-opening controls,
and with their familiar buzzing sound the
doors begin to swing open. A sudden
bright flash of lightning startles her, but
then she moves reluctantly towards the
open doorway.)*

Next Episode:
THE ESCAPE

EPISODE THREE

THE ESCAPE

1. THE TARDIS CONTROL ROOM (NIGHT).

(SUSAN *operates the door-opening controls, and with their familiar buzzing sound the doors begin to swing open. A sudden bright flash of lightning startles her, but then she moves reluctantly towards the open doorway.*)

2. THE JUNGLE CLEARING.

(SUSAN *steps out of the TARDIS. There is another flash of lightning, and she catches sight of a shadowy figure towering over her on an outcrop of rocks to her left. She sinks to the ground.*)

SUSAN: Who are you? What do you want?

ALYDON: Don't be afraid!

SUSAN: What do you want?

(ALYDON *steps into full view. He is not the mutation* SUSAN *was expecting, but rather a tall, handsome man with blond hair.*)

But they said you were . . . but they called you . . . you're not . . . you're perfect!

ALYDON:	I tried to speak to you in the forest, yesterday, but I frightened you. I'm sorry.
SUSAN:	I was frightened . . . I was terrified.
ALYDON:	Yes, I was very clumsy. I have come now to make certain you understand how to use the drugs I left for you.
SUSAN:	You left? But we thought they'd been dropped by accident.
ALYDON:	No.
SUSAN:	We didn't even know they were drugs.
ALYDON:	You mean you haven't taken them yet? But you must!
SUSAN:	That's why I came back, you see.

(*She starts to get up.*)

My Grandfather and two of my friends are prisoners in the city and . . .

ALYDON:	Oh, please, please, you're too quick for me.

(*He jumps down from the outcrop he has been standing on.*)

There are four of you, I know that, I've watched you. What do you mean . . . prisoners?

SUSAN:	Well, don't you know about the Daleks?
ALYDON:	So the Dalek people have survived, but . . . but do they live in that dead city?
SUSAN:	Well, underneath it anyway. You see, the Daleks want the drugs too, and they won't let us go until I bring them back to them.
ALYDON:	But why should they want the drugs? Surely they must have some themselves if they're still alive?
SUSAN:	I don't know, but my Grandfather and my friends are terribly ill. I must take the drug back to them, please!

ALYDON:	No, no, no, wait. Are you sure the Daleks want the drugs for your friends and not for themselves?
SUSAN:	I hadn't thought of that.
ALYDON:	Do you trust them?
SUSAN:	No! Well, I'm not sure.
ALYDON:	You still have the drugs I left for you. I shall give you a further supply which you must hide as best you can.

(*He advances further towards her, and then stops.*)

	Do you trust me?
SUSAN:	Yes.

(ALYDON *gives* SUSAN *a second batch of drugs.*)

ALYDON:	I am Alydon, of the Thal race. I shall go with you through the forest to the outer wall of the city, if you will allow me.
SUSAN:	Thank you. I don't understand . . . they said you were . . . well, they called you mutations.
ALYDON:	Here, take my cloak. You are cold.

(*He takes his cloak from his own shoulders and puts it round* SUSAN'*s shoulders. She gratefully accepts.*)

SUSAN:	Thank you.
ALYDON:	We are the survivors of a final war. But the radiation still persists and that is why your friends are ill. I wonder if the Daleks have seen us?
SUSAN:	Seen you?
ALYDON:	I mean, if they call us mutations, what must they be like?

3. THE DALEK CONTROL ROOM (DAY).

(*Two Daleks are studying various controls and instruments against a wall. A voice grates out from the console.*)

DALEK: (*OOV*) I have re-turned the girl to the cell.

DALEK ONE: Ve-ry well.

DALEK: (*OOV*) They are ask-ing for wa-ter.

DALEK ONE: Give them some.

(*He turns off the speaker.*)

It is clear that the girl must have made con-tact with the Thals.

DALEK TWO: Our pri-son-ers could bring the Thals to us.

DALEK ONE: Pre-cis-ely that.

4. THE CELL.

(SUSAN *is holding a metal cup to* THE DOCTOR'*s lips.* BARBARA *is also drinking. On the floor near* SUSAN *is* ALYDON'*s cape.*)

SUSAN: The Thal said the drug would act quickly.

(IAN *is on the other side of* THE DOCTOR, *who is barely conscious.*)

IAN: Don't give him any more water, Susan. His pulse is steady now, anyway.

(SUSAN *stops trying to force* THE DOCTOR *to drink any more water.*)

BARBARA: My arms are tingling.

SUSAN: Yes, Alydon said you'd feel that. It . . . It just means the drug's working, that's all.

IAN: This Alydon of yours seems to have kept his wits

about him. Giving you that extra supply of drugs.

SUSAN: Yes. It was strange when the Daleks found it. I thought first of all they were going to keep both lots. Then they suddenly seemed to change their minds, and gave the second lot back to me.

IAN: Yes. Still, the Thals seem more friendly.

SUSAN: Oh, yes, Alydon gave me this cloak to keep me warm.

BARBARA: Why do the Daleks think they're mutations?

SUSAN: I don't know. Judging by Alydon, they're magnificent people.

(THE DOCTOR *opens his eyes and calls out weakly.*)

THE DOCTOR: Susan . . .

SUSAN: Grandfather, you'll feel better soon. I brought the drugs back.

THE DOCTOR: Oh . . . give me a little while and then we must go back to the Ship.

SUSAN: No, we're still prisoners.

THE DOCTOR: Oh, are we? Oh, yes, well we . . . we must leave here soon. We must . . . we must leave, er must . . .

(THE DOCTOR *drifts off again into a light sleep.*)

SUSAN: As soon as Grandfather's properly awake, we must try and find a way of helping the Thals.

BARBARA: We can't even help ourselves, locked up in here like this.

SUSAN: We must try and talk to the Daleks. Alydon said the Thals are going to starve unless they can find new supplies of food.

(*A camera lens unobtrusively sited high in one corner of the cell is relaying this.*)

You see after the war, the Thals that survived managed to cultivate small plots of land. And, well, that's how they've survived ever since. But they've always had to be very, very careful, because the crops have always been in danger. But, you see they rely on a great rainfall that only happens about every four or five years. Well, it's two years overdue now, and all their crops are ruined . . .

5. THE DALEK CONTROL ROOM.

(SUSAN *can be seen on a view-screen.*)

SUSAN:	(*OOV*) . . . Well, that's why the whole Thal race had to leave their plateau and go in search of food. Alydon says unless we can help them – arrange some sort of treaty with the Daleks . . . well, they're all going to die.
IAN:	(*OOV*) But how can we, Susan?
SUSAN:	(*OOV*) Well, he wants to talk to the Daleks. He says if they agree to supply food for them, then one of us must take a message outside the city.

(*One of the listening Daleks turns off the speaker.*)

DALEK TWO:	We could let this cat-ast-ro-phe de-stroy the Thals.
DALEK ONE:	Will they let them-selves starve to death? No, I feel pre-serv-ing our pri-son-ers was a good id-e-a.
DALEK TWO:	And an ar-range-ment to bring the Thals in-side our ci-ty an ev-en bet-ter one.
DALEK ONE:	We'll let our pri-son-ers sleep and then give them food. Af-ter that we can plan.
DALEK TWO:	Why not be-gin now?

DALEK ONE: Be-cause the lapse of time, the re-lax-at-ion of sleep, the pro-vis-ion of food . . . all these things will give them a false sense of se-cur-ity.

6. THE CELL.

(All four travellers are asleep. It is several hours later. IAN wakes up at once as a slight sound can be heard outside the door. He wakes SUSAN as the door opens and a Dalek stands in the doorway. Its sucker-stick is holding out a small metal tray.)

DALEK: We have brought you food and more wa-ter.

(BARBARA and THE DOCTOR wake up.)

The girl is to come with me.

IAN: Why?

SUSAN: It's all right.

(SUSAN gets up and goes to the door.)

BARBARA: Well, what are they going to do to her?

DALEK: She will be re-turned. We are go-ing to help the Thals, which is what you want us to do. Come now.

(SUSAN goes out and the door closes after her.)

THE DOCTOR: I can't understand. Why have they taken Susan?

IAN: How do they know we want to help the Thals?

7. THE JUNGLE CLEARING.

(ALYDON is sitting on the rocky outcrop near the TARDIS. Several more Thals enter the clearing from the forest. There

are two young and handsome men, a beautiful young woman, DYONI, *and a regal-looking older man,* TEMMOSUS, *who is clearly their leader.*)

ALYDON: Ah, Ganatus!

GANATUS: Alydon!

ALYDON: You have been longer than I thought.

GANATUS: The path was rough.

ALYDON: The dead city lies over there.

TEMMOSUS: Place the tent here, towards the west.

(*They look at the TARDIS*).

DYONI: Well, what is it, Temmosus?

TEMMOSUS: This must be the craft in which the strangers arrived here. So, Alydon, we were right to believe the city inhabited.

ALYDON: Yes, Temmosus.

TEMMOSUS: I wonder what they'll be like? How they'll be disposed towards us?

GANATUS: They are Daleks.

TEMMOSUS: Yes, but we've changed over the centuries. Why shouldn't they? The once famous warrior race of Thals are now farmers.

DYONI: But the Daleks were teachers, weren't they, Temmosus?

TEMMOSUS: Yes, they were . . . and philosophers.

GANATUS: Perhaps they are the warriors now.

TEMMOSUS: From the distance, the city looks as if they make science and invention their profession. It's a magical architecture. Perhaps we can exchange ideas with them . . . learn from them.

GANATUS: Perhaps . . .

TEMMOSUS: And these others, they arrived here in this . . . weird object?

(*He points towards the TARDIS.*)

ALYDON: Yes, Temmosus.

TEMMOSUS: And you trust them, Alydon?

ALYDON: I have only spoken with the young girl, but if the others are anything like her, I would trust them absolutely.

TEMMOSUS: I hope you are not too generous in your beliefs. What do you say, Dyoni? Hm?

DYONI: I have no opinion on the matter.

(GANATUS *laughs mockingly.*)

GANATUS: How unusual!

TEMMOSUS: Where is the girl now?

ALYDON: I have given her the drugs, and she has returned to the city.

DYONI: It would have been better to have given it to a man instead of a girl.

ALYDON: Well, I had no choice. They're prisoners in the city.

GANATUS: Prisoners?

TEMMOSUS: Are you sure?

ALYDON: I'm afraid so. From everything the young girl said, the Daleks are certainly very suspicious of others.

TEMMOSUS: Tell me, Alydon, how old is this young girl?

ALYDON: Oh . . . no longer a child . . . not yet a woman.

TEMMOSUS: Ah, then perhaps it's safe for you to talk to her . . . if she's not yet a woman.

(*He laughs.* DYONI *moves away angrily.*)

ALYDON: I don't understand her. If we don't find a ne food supply for next year, we're finished. Doesn't she understand that? We're all working towards the same end.

GANATUS:	Now there's a double meaning for you!
TEMMOSUS:	But don't you realise that Dyoni sees her personal future in you? You must remember that when we left our plateau and started on this journey, she was little more than a child – but that was four years ago.
ALYDON:	I'm not quite so blind.
GANATUS:	Ha!
TEMMOSUS:	Well, go on, what have you planned?
ALYDON:	The young girl will speak with the Daleks. And the message will come from the city.
TEMMOSUS:	Direct from the girl?
ALYDON:	Yes.
TEMMOSUS:	But how shall we know that it is not a trick?
ALYDON:	She told me her name . . . Susan. And that is how the message is to be signed. Otherwise w shall know the Daleks are hostile to us.

8. *The Dalek Control Room.*

(SUSAN is seated at a small metal table. In front of her is a sheet of pliable soft metal. She is holding a stylus and is writing with it on the metal sheet. The Daleks face her and one of them is dictating.)

DALEK ONE:	. . . and li-quid foods. Wa-ter in ab-und-ance. We can al-so sup-ply un-lim-it-ed quan-ti-ties of fresh veg-et-a-bles, which are forced in art-if-ic-ial sun-light.
SUSAN:	Just a minute . . . art-if-ic-ial sun-light . . . All right, go on.
DALEK TWO:	In re-turn, we shall ex-pect the Thals to help us in the re-cul-ti-vat-ion of the land sur-round-ing the ci . . .

(The Dalek is interrupted as the other

Dalek notices that SUSAN *is not copying down the dictation.*)

DALEK ONE:	Why have you stopped writ-ing?
SUSAN:	Well, I can only ask them. I can't accept for them.
DALEK ONE:	Then put down that we ex-pect them to help us.
SUSAN:	Yes. I'm sure they will.

(*She finishes writing and lays down the stylus.*)

DALEK TWO:	Please sit still while we ex-am-ine what you have writ-ten.

(*The Dalek picks up the metal sheet with its sucker-stick.*)

DALEK ONE:	What is the last word here?
SUSAN:	The last word?
DALEK ONE:	Sew-san?

(SUSAN *giggles, which alarms the Daleks.*)

DALEK ONE:	Stop that noise!
SUSAN:	Well, it's . . . it's . . . it's what I'm called. It's my name. Susan.
DALEK ONE:	And you told the Thals that you would write this name on the mes-sage?
SUSAN:	Yes. Look, there's no need to be frightened of them. They're very friendly people. All they want is food. Let me take the message to them.
DALEK ONE:	No.
SUSAN:	Well, why not?
DALEK TWO:	We have planned . . . oth-er-wise.

(*Suddenly we hear* IAN'*s voice. The Daleks have activated their monitoring equipment.*)

IAN: (*OOV*) . . . but how long are they going to keep Susan, Doctor?

BARBARA: (*OOV*) What do they want with her?

THE DOCTOR: (*OOV*) Perhaps they're going to let us go. I don't know.

(*The Dalek turns the sound off.*)

SUSAN: We knew you could hear us, because you knew about the Thals and the food.

DALEK ONE: It does not mat-ter. We have the mes-sage now.

(SUSAN *realises what this might mean.*)

9. THE CELL.

(SUSAN *has been returned to the cell.* IAN *whispers to* THE DOCTOR.)

IAN: All set, Doctor.

(*Then he speaks louder.*)

The whole pattern of things is suspicious. Just because the Daleks didn't kill us, is no reason to trust them.

THE DOCTOR: Or suspect them, either.

BARBARA: Well, maybe they just have a different way of doing things.

IAN: The Thals have helped us. The Daleks put us in a cell. I know which of the two I prefer.

THE DOCTOR: I tell you the Daleks are brilliant people. I think we ought to co-operate with them.

IAN: Ever since you talked alone to the Daleks, you've been on their side. What have they done – bribed you, or something?

(IAN *grabs* THE DOCTOR.)

Look, I want to know why. Why are you on their side and against the rest of us?

THE DOCTOR: Take your hands off me! How dare you?

(*The two struggle.* BARBARA *and* SUSAN *join in the fight, all shouting.* SUSAN *jumps on* IAN's *shoulders, but it is just a ploy to enable her to grab the Daleks' spy-camera off the wall.*)

BARBARA: Susan, what are you doing?

(SUSAN *pulls the camera away, wires trailing from it, then she and* IAN *collapse to the ground.*

10. *THE DALEK CONTROL ROOM.*

(*The Daleks' viewing screen suddenly goes blank.*)

11. *THE CELL.*

IAN: Did I hurt you?

SUSAN: No.

THE DOCTOR: Don't waste time.

(IAN *looks at the broken camera in his hands.*)

IAN: That's fixed you for a while!

12. *THE DALEK CONTROL ROOM.*

DALEK ONE: Do you think it was bro-ken ac-cid-ent-al-ly in their strug-gle?

DALEK TWO: No. The ca-ble is strong. They have bro-ken it de-lib-er-ate-ly.

DALEK THREE: They can be moved im-med-i-at-ely to a-noth-er room; the eye re-paired.

DALEK ONE:	No.
DALEK TWO:	Ex-ter-mi-nat-ion then?
DALEK ONE:	There is no es-cape from the room that holds them. They may well be use-ful a-gain. We shall deal with the Thals.

13. *THE CELL.*

THE DOCTOR:	The point is, how do we get out of here? Wait until the Daleks open the door and force the issue?
BARBARA:	Oh, we'd never get near them.
SUSAN:	We must try and trick them. We must all pretend to be dead – then when they come in to investigate, we must rush down the corridor . . .
IAN:	Yes, and then what? No, we must find a way of putting these machines out of action.
BARBARA:	Yes, remember what they did to your legs!
IAN:	Yes.
THE DOCTOR:	The floors are metal . . . All the floors are metal.
BARBARA:	Well, so are the streets of the city, outside.
THE DOCTOR:	Why?
BARBARA:	I don't know.
THE DOCTOR:	No, I know you don't know. I mean why do they use metal? Is it because it lasts longer, or because . . .
IAN:	Because it's essential to them? That's an idea.
BARBARA:	Well, how is that going to help us?
IAN:	Well, if metal is elec . . .
THE DOCTOR:	No, no, no, no, no, no! Now listen, let's concentrate on the Daleks. Have you noticed, for example, that when they move about there's a sort of acrid smell?
SUSAN:	Yes, yes, I've noticed that.
BARBARA:	I know! A fairground.

IAN:	That's it! Dodgems . . .
THE DOCTOR:	It's electricity! I think they're powered that way.
IAN:	Yes, but just a minute! They have no pick-up or anything. And only the base of the machine touches the floor. How do they complete the circuit?
SUSAN:	Batteries?
THE DOCTOR:	No, no, no. I believe the Daleks have discovered a way to exploit static electricity. Very ingenious, if I'm right.
BARBARA:	What, drawing power from the floor.
THE DOCTOR:	Precisely . . . if I'm right, of course. Now what do we know, apart from guessing how they're powered. Hm?
SUSAN:	Well, they can see all round them.
BARBARA:	Yes . . . their eye is flexible, like a large camera lens.
THE DOCTOR:	Yes, yes, yes, yes. Now, Chesterton, do you mind concentrating, young man?
IAN:	Hm? Susan, the cloak the Thals gave you?
SUSAN:	Yes, it's just behind you.
IAN:	Barbara, come here. Now what do you think this is made of?
BARBARA:	Oh, I don't know. It isn't plastic, and I don't think it's nylon either.
IAN:	Whatever it is, it'll do for what we want.
THE DOCTOR:	And what will it do, young man? Hm?
IAN:	Insulate. If you are right, Doctor, about the Daleks taking up power from the floor, this is a perfect way of putting them out of action.

14. THE JUNGLE CLEARING.

(DYONI *is talking to* GANATUS.)

DYONI:	Oh, look, Ganatus, they've found a magnadon under some bushes.

(*She indicates the creature* THE DOCTOR *said was made of metal.*)

GANATUS: Dead, I hope?

DYONI: Well, of course it's dead.

(*She realises too late that he is teasing her.*)

Oh, I never know when you are serious and when you are joking.

GANATUS: We'll be able to recharge the hand-lights. I'll go and tell Antodus.

DYONI: Is he still afraid of the dark? Oh, I'm sorry, I . . .

GANATUS: My brother isn't afraid of anything.

(*Nearby,* ALYDON *is discussing the situation with* TEMMOSUS.)

ALYDON: Temmosus, suppose the Daleks refuse to help us. What then?

TEMMOSUS: I believe the Daleks hold the key to our future. Whatever that future may be, we must accept it, gracefully and without regret.

ALYDON: I wish I could be as objective as you. We've lived for so long a time.

TEMMOSUS: Perhaps we have lived too long. I've never struggled against the inevitable – that's a vain occupation – but I should always advise you to examine very closely what you think to be inevitable. It's surprising how often apparent defeat can be turned to victory.

(GANATUS *comes over to them, clutching* SUSAN'*s message. He gives it to* TEMMOSUS.)

GANATUS: This was found at the city gates.

ALYDON: What does it say?

TEMMOSUS: They're going to help us! It is signed by the girl,

Susan. She says the Dalek people have no malice toward us, and they hope that they can work with us to build a new and safe world, free from the fear of war. They have the ability to produce food by means of synthetic sunlight, and they have left a quantity of it for us in the entrance hall of their main building. We are to collect it tomorrow.

> (*By now a large group of Thals has gathered round to hear this, and there is a good deal of excited chatter amongst them.*)

So there is a future for us.

15. THE CELL.

> (SUSAN *stands with her ear pressed against the door. She waves her hand violently at the others, who are talking.*)

SUSAN: Ssssh! He's coming!

THE DOCTOR: Ready?

IAN: Yes.

THE DOCTOR: Now, all of you, watch very carefully. See that you notice every detail on that machine. Right?

> (*The door slides open and a Dalek stands in the corridor, eyeing them warily.* IAN *is close by the doorway, looking at the floor with immense interest.*)

DALEK: Move back from the door.

> (IAN *moves back.*)

DALEK: Take the food.

> (SUSAN *moves forward and takes the tray. The Dalek moves backwards and shuts the*

door. The others remain silent until they are sure he has gone and cannot hear them.)

THE DOCTOR: Well?

IAN: I'll be able to jam the door with a piece of this.

(*He holds up the broken camera.*)

SUSAN: They seem to be able to cover all of us.

BARBARA: It's impossible to hide from it.

IAN: Yes, perhaps we could throw a coat over the lens.

BARBARA: Surely it would see you?

IAN: Yes . . . Doctor, perhaps we can stage something? You know, a distraction, and when the lens looks the other way – throw something over it.

THE DOCTOR: Yes, yes, yes, yes.

BARBARA: Now wait a minute. Susan, throw me your shoes.

(SUSAN *does so.*)

IAN: What are you up to?

(BARBARA *is busy scraping the undersides of the shoes over one of the almost empty water bowls.*)

BARBARA: Making mud!

16. THE CELL (LATER THAT DAY.)

(THE DOCTOR *checks his watch.*)

THE DOCTOR: If he's on time, we have three minutes.

(IAN *is busy breaking off a piece of the camera.*)

IAN: I'm ready.

(IAN *moves to the doorway. He crouches down on the floor, hard against the side of the door.*)

THE DOCTOR: How's the mud?

(BARBARA *is busy kneading of ball of mud in her hands.*)

BARBARA: Oh, it's very sticky and very nasty.

THE DOCTOR: Yes, good . . . a very good idea.

SUSAN: Shall I spread the cape open?

THE DOCTOR: Yes, yes, not too near the door. We don't want to make him suspicious.

(SUSAN *spreads the cape out on to the middle of the cell floor.*)

SUSAN: Just down there?

THE DOCTOR: Yes, yes, quickly . . . hurry, child!

(*A sound catches* IAN's *attention.*)

IAN: He's coming!

(*They all stand tensed in their positions. As the door starts to open,* IAN *jams the metal under in the doorway and retreats before the door opens still further. The door continues to open and the Dalek stands before them holding a food tray. It directs its attention towards* SUSAN.)

DALEK: Take this.

(SUSAN *gets up from the floor and moves to take the tray.* BARBARA *advances slightly towards the doorway.* SUSAN *puts the tray down quite near the door. The Dalek presses the control to close the door and it starts to slide shut. When it is almost closed, it hits* IAN's *piece of metal. The mechanism whirrs briefly, trying to overcome the obstacle, and then the door opens again. The Dalek eyes the cause of the malfunction, and extends its suckerstick to remove it.*)

THE DOCTOR: Now!

(*The Dalek's eye-piece swings upwards as* BARBARA *dashes forward and slaps the ball of mud directly on to the lens. The Dalek's sucker- and gun-sticks flail blindly.*)

IAN: Back!

DALEK: Keep a-way! Keep a-way from me! Keep a-way from me. Keep a-way. Keep a-way!

(THE DOCTOR *and* IAN *move towards the machine.* IAN *is pinned to the wall by the Dalek's sucker-stick, but together with* THE DOCTOR *he tries desperately to drag the Dalek into the cape.*)

IAN: Mind the gun, the gun!

DALEK: Keep a-way! Keep a-way from me! Keep a-way from me. Keep a-way from me. Keep a-way from me!

(*The Dalek puts up a terrific fight, but without its eye-piece, is at a disadvantage.* BARBARA *joins in, trying to shove the Dalek on to the cape, and eventually their* _combined efforts succeed. At once the Dalek's arms all go limp. The others realise breathlessly that they have won._)

SUSAN: Yes, we've got it!

THE DOCTOR: Well done, Susan!

BARBARA: Ian?

THE DOCTOR: Are you all right, Susan?

SUSAN: Yes, Grandfather.

THE DOCTOR: Splendid, splendid!

IAN: I think I'm all right. Swing it round. Keep out of the way, Susan.

SUSAN: Yes.

IAN: Now . . . I think it's worked. Take your hand off the gun . . . It has, it's worked! Now, there must be a catch here somewhere.

(_He feels around for one._)

I've found one!

(IAN _starts to pull open the Dalek's hinged top. As he does so there is a sickening, slurping sound from inside._ IAN _catches sight of the Dalek's contents and quickly closes it again._)

Susan, Barbara! Go in that corridor and keep a look-out.

BARBARA: Yes.

(IAN _waits until_ SUSAN _and_ BARBARA _have moved away, then looks at_ THE DOCTOR.)

IAN: You'll have to help me.

(_He opens the lid again and_ THE DOCTOR _is also repelled by the contents._)

Let's roll it off the cloak.

(*They do so.*)

All right?

THE DOCTOR: Yes.

IAN: Give me the cloak.

(*He moves the Dalek slightly to release the cloak.*)

IAN: That's it. All right?

THE DOCTOR: Right.

(*Together they manoeuvre the cloak down into the Dalek casing and use it to remove the contents.*)

IAN: Right, now . . . lift!

(THE DOCTOR *takes the bundle and puts it in a corner of the cell.*)

Now . . . see if I can get inside it. All clear in the corridor?

BARBARA
AND SUSAN: Yes.

SUSAN: I think there's a sentry down the other end of the corridor.

BARBARA: Well, they've made such a terrible noise. Ian, hurry!

(IAN *manages with difficulty to squeeze himself into the Dalek casing.*)

IAN: Not much room for my legs, but . . . try the top.

THE DOCTOR: Barbara, Susan! Give me a hand. Let it down gently.

(*Together they lower the top half of the Dalek.*)

THE DOCTOR: How is it?

IAN: It's very cramped indeed.

(*His voice is now distorted like a Dalek's, but still carries the tell-tale inflections of a human voice.*)

THE DOCTOR: Well, can't you sound more like a Dalek?

BARBARA: Yes, in a monotone. You've heard them.

(IAN *does his best to imitate them.*)

IAN: Do . . . you . . . mean . . . like . . . this?

SUSAN: Ha! That's marvellous! Can you see all right?

IAN: No, there's some sort of screen . . . Oh, it's the mud. Wipe the mud off the lens.

SUSAN: Oh yes, all right. Eurgh! It's all clogged up. Is that better?

(*With a handkerchief, she wipes most of it off.*)

IAN: Yes, yes, I can see now. But I can't make this thing move. It . . . it's full of controls.

THE DOCTOR: Oh, don't worry, we'll push you.

IAN: Well, it moves well enough.

BARBARA: Yes, but surely they'll know that we're pushing you?

THE DOCTOR: Oh no, no, no, they won't be suspicious at all.

IAN: All right now, Susan, Barbara. You get in front and pretend I'm taking you for questioning.

SUSAN: Right!

BARBARA: Yes.

IAN: And, Susan?

SUSAN: Yes?

IAN: You lead us, you know the way.

SUSAN: All right, it's this way then.

(*As they move off out of the cell, the bundle in the corner twitches and, as part of the cape slips off, a large glistening webbed claw, reminiscent of a giant frog can be seen. It clenches and unclenches, then lies still.*)

Next Episode:
THE AMBUSH

THE AMBUSH

1. The Cell (Day).

IAN: And, Susan?

SUSAN: Yes?

IAN: You lead us, you know the way.

SUSAN: All right. It's this way then.

> (*As they move off, the bundle in the corner of the cell twitches and, as part of the cape slips off, a large glistening webbed claw reminiscent of a giant frog can be seen. It clenches and unclenches, then lies still.*)

2. A Corridor.

IAN: Hey, let go a minute! I think I've found out how to operate this thing. Yes, I can! Quick Doctor, get in front! Ready? Off we go!

SUSAN: Wait! This looks like the place.

> (*She goes ahead and peers gingerly around a corner, then goes back to the others.*)

There's a great iron door, with a Dalek on guard. And beyond the door there's a lift.

> (*As they turn the corner they see a Dalek*)

standing guard beside a control panel. Beyond the Dalek is the door, which is closed.)

THE DOCTOR: It's up to you now, Chesterton. Do as little talking as possible.

IAN: All right.

(*The group move towards the Dalek guard. As they approach, it swings towards them.*)

DALEK: Stop!

IAN: The coun-cil wish-es to ques-tion the pri-son-ers.

DALEK: I have not been in-formed. Wait.

(*The Dalek moves to the control panel.* THE DOCTOR *and* BARBARA *stand frozen to the spot. In a flash of inspiration,* SUSAN *suddenly breaks away, shouting at the top of her voice.*)

SUSAN: No, I'm not going, no . . .

IAN: Hold her!

(*The real Dalek moves quickly to hold* SUSAN, *who winks conspiratorially at the others.*)

DALEK: I have got her. Now hold still.

IAN: Help me to get them in-side.

(*While* IAN – *in his Dalek guise* – *holds* SUSAN, *the real Dalek operates the door-opening mechanism, and* SUSAN *is pushed roughly into the room beyond.*)

You too.

(*The others follow.*)

3. THE LIFT ANTE-ROOM.

DALEK: Shall I help you to the fourth le-vel with them?

IAN: No. Close the doors. The girl can-not run far in-side.

(*The Dalek moves back out of the ante-room. It presses a button and the door slides shut. The moment it is fully closed,* THE DOCTOR *rushes over to it and pulls at a cable leading into a box near the base of the door. It comes away in his hand.*)

THE DOCTOR: That's fixed the door!

BARBARA: That was a very good idea, Susan.

IAN: He didn't hurt you?

SUSAN: No. Not really.

IAN: Well, help me to get out of this thing. I'm suffocating.

BARBARA: Right. Hang on.

(BARBARA *and* THE DOCTOR *move to the back of the Dalek and try to release* IAN.)

The clasp is stuck.

THE DOCTOR: Here, let me help fix it.

4. THE CORRIDOR.

(*The Dalek guard is speaking into a microphone on the control panel.*)

DALEK: I have just passed the pri-son-ers through in-to lift shaft se-ven.

(*There is a brief moment's pause, whilst the Dalek at the other end checks this.*)

DALEK: (*OOV*) There are no or-ders to move the pri-son-ers. Hold them.

(*The Dalek quickly presses the door-opening control. There is a whirring sound, but the door stays firmly shut.*)

DALEK: The door is locked. E-mer-gen-cy al-arm!

(*The Dalek presses another control, and an alarm klaxon immediately starts to sound. Two other Daleks arrive.*)

DALEK: (*OOV*) At-tent-ion. Im-mob-il-ize lift shaft se-ven. Floor ar-ea . . .

5. *THE LIFT ANTE-ROOM.*

(BARBARA *and* THE DOCTOR *are still trying to open the Dalek casing. They hear the alarm bells.*)

IAN: They know! Come on . . . hurry up, will you?

THE DOCTOR: Wait a minute . . . There, it's free. Lift its lid off.

SUSAN: Hurry up!

(BARBARA *and* THE DOCTOR *are still unable to open the Dalek's casing.*)

BARBARA: I . . . I can't move it . . . it won't budge!

THE DOCTOR: Chesterton, try and force it up from the inside.

IAN: I'm trying. No, no, it's no good. There's something jammed inside here. Forcing it is only making it worse.

(*From the other side of the door, we hear something bang against the door.*)

BARBARA: Ian, come on . . . hurry!

IAN: I . . . I can't move it!

(SUSAN, *who is standing by the door,*

listening, rests her hand against it. Suddenly she yells with pain and snatches her hand away.)

SUSAN:	Hey! The door's red-hot!
THE DOCTOR:	They're cutting through the door.
BARBARA:	We'll have to move you into the lift.
THE DOCTOR:	Yes, well hurry, hurry!
SUSAN:	It's stuck!
BARBARA:	I don't understand it, it moved easily enough before.
THE DOCTOR:	They've magnetised the floor. You feel it?
BARBARA:	Are you sure?
THE DOCTOR:	Yes . . . Chesterton, we're not able to get you into the lift.
IAN:	Yes, I realise that. Take the others away in the lift, Doctor.
BARBARA:	We're not going without you.
IAN:	Don't waste time, go on!
THE DOCTOR:	Well, come on, he's right.
BARBARA:	No, I'm not leaving Ian!
THE DOCTOR:	When we get to the top, we'll send the lift back down for you, all right?
SUSAN:	No, Grandfather, we can't!
IAN:	Go on . . . go on!
SUSAN:	No!
IAN:	Go on!
THE DOCTOR:	Come on, Susan!
IAN:	Barbara, for goodness sake, go!
SUSAN:	Oh, no!

(THE DOCTOR, followed by a reluctant SUSAN and BARBARA, gets into the lift. SUSAN points in horror at the door of the ante-room. The Daleks are cutting through,

and a charred line is rapidly growing as the flame-cutters do their work. THE DOCTOR *presses a control and the lift starts to rise.* IAN, *inside the Dalek casing, desperately tries to free himself.*)

IAN: I must . . . must get out!

6. *THE CORRIDOR.*

(*The Daleks are still busily cutting through the door.*)

7. *INSIDE THE LIFT.*

BARBARA: How long will it take them to cut through?

THE DOCTOR: Oh, maybe ten minutes. If we're lucky, longer.

SUSAN: But even if he does get out, he's stuck down there. The only way out is the lift. We must go back for him.

(*She lunges at the control buttons, but* THE DOCTOR *restrains her.*)

THE DOCTOR: Susan, it's no good! We cannot do anything for him now, child.

8. *THE LIFT SHAFT.*
(*The lift continues to rise rapidly up the shaft.*)

9. *THE CORRIDOR.*

(*The Dalek cutting through the door moves steadily round, only a few inches remain uncut.*)

10. *THE LIFT SHAFT.*

(*The lift continues to rise, and then stops.*)

11. INSIDE THE LIFT.

(*The lift has reached the top. As the three travellers step out,* THE DOCTOR *presses a control and the lift sinks from sight.*)

BARBARA: We should never have left him. It's so slow. It'll never reach him in time.

12. THE LIFT SHAFT.

(*The lift descends the lift shaft.*)

13. THE CORRIDOR.

DALEK: It is near-ly com-ple-ted.

(*The two other Daleks move close to the door, as the last remaining inches are burnt away.*)

14. THE LIFT ANTE-ROOM.

(*Suddenly the door falls inwards. The Daleks swarm into the room, firing mercilessly at the Dalek within until the whole of one side is blasted away. One of the Daleks moves forwards and pushes it. It collapses in on itself.*)

DALEK ONE: It is emp-ty.
DALEK TWO: Lock the lift!
DALEK ONE: The em-erg-en-cy switch. Bring it down!

(*The second Dalek moves across to the control panel. From the indicator lights, it can be seen that the lift is nearly at the top again.*)

15. THE LIFT SHAFT.

(*The lift continues to rise up the shaft.*)

16. *The Upper Lift Room.*

(THE DOCTOR, SUSAN *and* BARBARA *anxiously watch the lift level indicator.*)

BARBARA: Come on, Ian . . . come on!

IAN: (*OOV*) All right, I'm coming!

(*The indicator continues to climb, but with agonizing slowness. Finally the lift-cage starts to appear, then halts and starts to descend again.* IAN *leaps for the floor,* BARBARA *grabs him and drags him up into the room, the roof of the lift narrowly missing his legs.*)

IAN: They had about two inches of that door to cut through when I got out.

SUSAN: Are you all right?

IAN: Yes, thank you, Susan.

THE DOCTOR: Well, never mind that now . . . we must try and find a way out of this room.

(*Across the other side of the room,* BARBARA *spots a window.*)

BARBARA: Daylight!

IAN: Yes. Well, where exactly are we?

THE DOCTOR: We're right at the top of the building. I can just see the surface of the city. See over there? There's the exit to the petrified jungle.

IAN: Yes, I'm trying to recognise the streets we came along.

BARBARA: Everything looks so different from above. Do you see anything at all that looks fa . . .

(*She breaks off.*)

IAN: What is it?

BARBARA:	Ian!
IAN:	What's the matter?
BARBARA:	There's someone down there. Look, by that sort of gateway thing beyond the low building. I saw someone cross that space.
THE DOCTOR:	A Dalek?
BARBARA:	No, it was a man . . . a human being.
SUSAN:	The Thals! They've come for food supplies.
THE DOCTOR:	Walking into an ambush.

17. *The Lift Ante-Room.*

DALEK ONE:	Make no at-tempt to cap-ture them. They are to be ex-ter-min-at-ed. You un-der-stand? Ex-ter-min-at-ed.
DALEK TWO:	I un-der-stand.

(*The first Dalek operates the lift control and, again it, rises out of sight.*)

18. *The Lift Shaft.*

(*The lift rises up the shaft once more.*)

19. *The Upper Lift Room.*

(*From outside the room, the four companions are desperately pounding on the glass window, and shouting to try to attract the attention of the unsuspecting Thals below. However, nothing can be heard through the window.*)

20. *The Upper Lift Room.*

(IAN *turns away from the window in despair.*)

IAN:	Oh, it's no good, this room must be sound-proof. We must find a way of getting down there.

THE DOCTOR:	Yes, but how, dear boy?
BARBARA:	Isn't this a door?
IAN:	Yes . . . Doctor, open it.
THE DOCTOR:	Oh, yes.

(*The door won't budge.*)

SUSAN:	What's the matter with it?
THE DOCTOR:	Oh, they've magnetised it too. Come on, let's try and force it open.
IAN:	I can get my fingers in it . . . hurry, yes . . . it's beginning to move.

(BARBARA *suddenly notices that the lift indicator lights are rising again.*)

BARBARA:	Ian, the lift is coming back!
SUSAN:	Oh, no!
IAN:	Doctor, keep working at the door.

21. THE LIFT SHAFT.

(*The lift continues to rise.*)

22. INTERIOR UPPER LIFT ROOM.

(IAN *presses some of the controls by the entrance to the lift shaft, but this has no effect.*)

IAN:	It's no good!

(*He looks desperately around the room. The only movable object in the entire room is a large kind of abstract statue in one corner. He crosses quickly over to it and tries to push it. It moves slightly, and then stops.*)

Come over here, give me a hand.

(*They do so.*)

Quick, now . . . all push together!

(*With a concerted effort, they manage to
slide the statue towards the lift shaft.* THE
DOCTOR *meanwhile is still at the door,
trying to open it.*)

THE DOCTOR: It's open! I've got it!
IAN: Be right with you.
THE DOCTOR: What are you doing?
IAN: Just cutting down the odds a bit. Are you ready,
now!
THE DOCTOR: What are you . . .
IAN: One . . . Two . . . Three . . . Push.

(*They all heave at once, and the statue
goes hurtling down the lift shaft.*)

23. THE LIFT SHAFT.

(*The statue tumbles down, bouncing off
the sides of the lift shaft. It hits the
ascending lift with a resounding crash.*)

24. THE LIFT ANTE-ROOM.

(*Several large pieces of rubble fall down;
the two remaining Daleks at the base of
the lift are engulfed in a cloud of dust and
debris.*)

25. THE UPPER LIFT ROOM.

(IAN *is struggling to hold the door open.*)

IAN: All right Doctor, through you go there. Go on!

26. *A Corridor.*

(ALYDON *comes cautiously into view. He looks warily about him. A few moments later* TEMMOSUS *joins him. They whisper to each other.*)

TEMMOSUS: You're much too suspicious.

ALYDON: Perhaps I am, Temmosus. But why should the Daleks help us?

TEMMOSUS: You've been saying that ever since their message arrived. Perhaps their offer was coldly worded, but friendship grows with time. These Daleks must have believed that they were the only survivors on this planet.

ALYDON: And are they relieved to find they aren't? Or are they shocked and horrified – perhaps insanely jealous?

TEMMOSUS: You've no reason to say that. I think you misjudge them.

ALYDON: Well, yes, I'm being illogical . . . unfair, if you like, but . . . I just have an instinct.

TEMMOSUS: Listen, we must find a new source of food. The Daleks have it, they've offered it to us. These are facts, Alydon, facts.

ALYDON: Yes, yes, I know. But let me talk to them.

TEMMOSUS: It's right that I should do so.

ALYDON: But supposing . . .

TEMMOSUS: No, Alydon! And you must throw off these suspicions. They're based on fear, and fear breeds hatred, and war. I shall speak to them peacefully, they'll see that I'm unarmed . . . there's no better argument against war than that.

(TEMMOSUS *moves out into the open, leaving* ALYDON *alone.*)

ALYDON: Yes . . . if they really want to listen.

27. THE RECEPTION HALL.

(*Piled in the middle of the room are boxes
and cartons. At first glance the hall appears
to be empty, but was we see around it,
there are Daleks in all the doorways and
recesses.*)

DALEK: They are ap-proach-ing.

(*The Daleks glide back into hiding. The
room appears deserted.*)

28. A CORRIDOR.

(*There is the sound of running footsteps
and then* IAN *bursts into view, followed by
the others.*)

SUSAN: Oh, Grandfather, come on. Come on, hurry!
BARBARA: Where are we?
IAN: By the city wall, I think. Yes, there's a gateway
              about fifty yards away.
BARBARA: Are there any Daleks?
IAN: Wait there . . .

(*He peers cautiously around a corner.*)

              No . . . no I think we're all right.
THE DOCTOR: Well, let's go back to the Ship.
SUSAN: No, no! We must warn the Thals!
THE DOCTOR: Susan!
THE DOCTOR: We can't let them walk into a trap.
THE DOCTOR: The Thals are no concern of ours. We cannot
              jeopardise our lives by getting involved in an
              affair which is none of our business.
BARBARA: Of course it's our business! The Thals gave us

the anti-radiation drug. Without that we'd be dead!

IAN: Yes, but the Doctor's got a point. There's no sense in risking our whole party.

SUSAN: No!

IAN: You go back to the Ship . . . I'll stay and warn the Thals.

SUSAN: No! We're all in this together. We're all going to stay here.

IAN: Susan, you do as I say. You go back to the ship with Barbara and your Grandfather.

SUSAN: But don't you understand . . .

BARBARA: I know what Ian means. He stands a much better chance on his own if he doesn't have us to worry about. Now, come on. We'll wait for you.

IAN: I'll be there.

THE DOCTOR: Good luck, Chesterton.

IAN: Thank you. Go on.

(SUSAN *is still reluctant to leave but* BARBARA *makes her go.* IAN *watches them for a moment, and then goes off to warn the Thals.*)

29. *THE RECEPTION HALL.*

(*The Daleks are still half-hidden in the various recesses. At a given signal they all pull further back and glide out of sight. Led by* TEMMOSUS, *the Thals approach. They halt in the doorway and* TEMMOSUS *advances alone into the centre of the room.*)

30. *A CORRIDOR.*

(IAN *reaches the ambush area.*)

31. THE RECEPTION HALL.

TEMMOSUS: Daleks! Can you hear me? Daleks! The Thal people wish to live in peace. If this is your wish too, then let us work together to rebuild our world.

> (*Hidden from view, the Daleks train their weapons on* TEMMOSUS.)

We need your help, and in return we'll make the soil live again. Grow crops, build homes. The time for enmity is past.

> (IAN *waits. He senses something is about to happen.*)

If this is the kind of future that you want, then send for us and we shall talk. You need not decide now. We have been waiting for centuries. We shall go on waiting.

> (*Behind him the Daleks silently glide from their hiding places.* TEMMOSUS *turns to his fellow Thals and indicates the boxes.*)

Take these things.

> (IAN *sees the Daleks emerging from their hiding places and can wait no longer.*)

IAN: No! It's a trap! Get out of here! Run!

> (TEMMOSUS *whirls around and suddenly sees the Daleks.*)

DALEK: Fire!

> (*The Thals in the doorway scatter confusedly.* TEMMOSUS *is hit by the Dalek's fire and collapses dead amongst the piles of food, spreading them all over the floor.*

IAN *sees a Dalek taking aim at him and ducks back behind a corner as the Dalek fires. The wall beside him blisters and bubbles.* IAN *runs off down the corridor. The Daleks are still firing at the fleeing Thals, but eventually they stop.* ALYDON *is hidden in a recess and the Daleks do not notice him. One of the Daleks moves towards the centre of the room and, with its eye-piece, looks down at the fallen body of* TEMMOSUS.)

32. *A Corridor.*

(IAN *cautiously opens a door, behind which he has been hiding. As he moves out into the open, he runs into* ALYDON.)

IAN: Who are you?

ALYDON: I am Alydon. You . . . you are the man who warned us.

IAN: Yes, I'm sorry I was late.

ALYDON: Yes, our . . . our leader Temmosus is dead.

IAN: I know, I saw it.

ALYDON: Why? Why kill him? They . . . they didn't even know him!

IAN: We can't stand here discussing it. Get yourself and your men away from here. Come on.

33. *The Jungle Clearing (Evening).*

(*The Thals have made camp around the area where the TARDIS landed. They sit together in silent groups, unable to take in what has happened. A young Thal woman looks questioningly at one of the male Thals who is keeping a lookout.*)

THAL: No, not yet.

(*On the ground nearby is a large metal capsule containing books, documents and various canisters.* THE DOCTOR *and* DYONI *are nearby.*)

THE DOCTOR: Fascinating. Absolutely fascinating! You know, these records must go back nearly a half a million years.

DYONI: The complete history of our planet Skaro is here. It seems now that no one will survive to read it.

THE DOCTOR: Oh, nonsense, young lady! Your survival is . . . is all here.

(*He points at one of several hexagonal plates which are lying together on the floor and together depict a map of the stars.*)

What, er . . . is this a solar system?

DYONI: Yes. Skaro is the twelfth planet. Here.

(*She points.*)

THE DOCTOR: I see . . . and this, this? What is this planet?

(*He points to a planet in the lower right-hand corner of the plate.*)

DYONI: Each of these maps has a tiny section of another solar system, so that a total picture can be built up.

THE DOCTOR: Total? Oh, you have records of other systems?

DYONI: Yes . . . well, I say total – of course we were only able to map out as far as our electroscopes allowed.

THE DOCTOR: Yes, I see. I wonder if I could see the plans?

DYONI: Oh, yes.

THE DOCTOR: I might be able to fix our position.

(DYONI *produces more of the metal plates.*)

Ah yes, yes. Absorbing, most absorbing.

(*He chuckles to himself.*)

34. *The Other Side of the Clearing.*

(SUSAN *and* BARBARA *are quietly talking.* IAN *stands nearby, silent and thoughtful.*)

SUSAN: Grandfather seems to be enjoying himself.

(ALYDON *comes up to* IAN.)

ALYDON: Some of the children have heard something moving in the forest.

IAN: It can't be the Daleks. They told us they couldn't come out of the city.

ALYDON: Nevertheless, I think we should all be on our guard.

(*Just then there is a shout, and the two brothers* ANTODUS *and* GANATUS *come into view.*)

LOOKOUT
THAL: Here they are! Antodus has been wounded.

GANATUS: We had to go round the other side of the city.

ALYDON: Is he badly hurt?

GANATUS: It's his shoulder.

BARBARA: I'll get some ointment and something to cover the burns.

SUSAN: Oh, we've got some in the Ship.

BARBARA: There's some over here.

GANATUS: We tried to go back for Temmosus.

LOOKOUT: (*OOV*) Temmosus? What's happened to Temmosus?

GANATUS:	It was hopeless.
ALYDON:	These are the people the Daleks were holding prisoner. And this is the man who shouted to warn us.
GANATUS:	Thank you. Did the others get away, Alydon?
ALYDON:	Tacanda was killed.

> (*There are gasps from the others when they hear this.*)

The rest of us escaped.

BARBARA:	The burns don't seem to be too bad. I'll get some water for him to drink. Can you manage?
DYONI:	Yes.
GANATUS:	Have you decided what we're going to do, Alydon? You must take the place of Temmosus now.
ALYDON:	Yes, yes, I know. If only I knew why the Daleks hated us. If I knew that I . . . I could alter our approach to them, perhaps.
IAN:	Your leader, Temmosus?
ALYDON:	Yes?
IAN:	Well, he appealed very sensibly to them. Any reasonable human beings would have responded to him. The Daleks didn't. They obviously think and act and feel in an entirely different way. They just aren't human.
GANATUS:	Yes, but why destroy without any apparent thought or reason? That's what I don't understand.
IAN:	Oh, there's a reason. Explanation might be better. It's stupid and ridiculous, but it's the only one that fits.
ALYDON:	What?
IAN:	A dislike for the unlike.
ALYDON:	But . . . I don't follow you.

IAN: They're afraid of you because you are different from them. So whatever you do, it doesn't matter.

DYONI: What would you have . . fight against them?

IAN: I didn't say that. But you must teach them to respect you. Show them some strength.

DYONI: But you really believe we ought to fight?

IAN: Yes, I think it may have to come to that.

DYONI: You understand as little about us as the Daleks do.

IAN: (*to* ALYDON) What would you do if the Daleks could leave their city? If they came up here and attacked you?

ALYDON: We would go away. Back to our plateau where we came from.

BARBARA: You'd simply run away?

(ALYDON *is disturbed by this comment.*)

IAN: Alydon, you can't go on running away. There are some things worth preserving.

GANATUS: We're not afraid to die. Temmosus proved that.

IAN: I am not talking about dying. Look, you can't hand yourselves over to the Daleks. Sooner or later they're going to try and destroy you if they can.

ALYDON: I can see you want to help us, but as Dyoni says, you . . . you don't understand. There can never be any question of the Thals fighting the Daleks. Come, Ganatus.

(*They leave* IAN *and* BARBARA *alone.*)

BARBARA: I don't understand them. They're not cowards, they don't seem to be afraid. Can pacifism become a human instinct?

IAN: Pacifism? Is that it? Pacifism only works when everybody feels the same.

BARBARA: Yes, but are they really pacifists? I mean genuinely so? Or is it a belief that's become a reality because they've never had to prove it?

(THE DOCTOR *bustles over to them.*)

THE DOCTOR: I say, I say! I think these will interest you. Look here.

(*He is holding a picture of a man – short and ugly, but powerfully built.*)

This is these people's ancestor. The original Thal male. There was a neutron war here. Most died and the survivors mutated. But in the case of the Thals, mutation came round in full circle, then refined itself into what you see.

IAN: You mean, this became . . .

(*He looks from the picture to the nearby group of Thals.*)

THE DOCTOR: Yes, yes. It took hundreds of years, of course. In the second example – our recent hosts – the mutation has not completed its full circle. Why I . . . I . . . I . . . don't know. But do you remember that monstrosity we took out of its machine?

IAN: Yes.

THE DOCTOR: This was its forebear.

(IAN *looks at a second picture.*)

IAN: Original Dalek.

THE DOCTOR: Yes. They called them Dals then. Oh, it's all there, every moment of it, Skaroine history. Minutely but brilliantly recorded. Priceless, absolutely priceless!

(IAN *pauses for a second, then picks up the first picture again.*)

IAN: Is this a sword the Thal's holding?

THE DOCTOR: Yes, they were the warriors then.

BARBARA: Were they?

THE DOCTOR: Undoubtedly.

(SUSAN *joins the group.*)

SUSAN: Antodus is feeling much better.

THE DOCTOR: Oh, I'm very glad to hear he's improving. Well, now, I'm sure you'll all agree with me, it's time we went back to the Ship. Now, come along.

SUSAN: Oh, Grandfather, couldn't we stay a bit longer? The Thals are such nice people.

THE DOCTOR: And the Daleks are not, which is more important, my child.

(*As he speaks, the body of* TEMMOSUS *is being brought past by some Thals.*)

IAN: I wonder if there's any point in reminding the Thals of what they used to be?

THE DOCTOR: Why?

BARBARA: Oh, they're opposed to fighting. We were trying to convince them that it was a necessity for their own survival.

THE DOCTOR: But our fate doesn't rest with the Thals, surely? Let's leave well alone – we have ourselves to worry about. Now, come along, come along.

IAN: Maybe the Doctor's right.

BARBARA: Yes, let's get in the Ship and get as far away from here as possible.

THE DOCTOR: Oh, please, come along. Oh, by the way, let me have the fluid link, will you?

(*As* IAN *starts to fumble for the link, realisation dawns on him.*)

Oh, dear boy, now please, please come along. You know I can't start the Ship without it.

IAN: The fluid link . . .

SUSAN: You've lost it?

BARBARA: But you can't have!

IAN: No. The Daleks took it from me when they searched me. It's down there somewhere . . . in the city.

Next Episode:
THE EXPEDITION

EPISODE FIVE

THE EXPEDITION

1. THE JUNGLE CLEARING .

IAN: The fluid link . . .

SUSAN: You've lost it?

BARBARA: Ian, you can't have!

IAN: No. The Daleks took it from me when they
            searched me. It must be down there somewhere
            . . . in the city.

*2. THE DALEK CONTROL ROOM
(NIGHT).*

(A Dalek enters the control room.)

DALEK TWO: The drug has been du-plic-at-ed.

DALEK ONE: And the dis-trib-ut-ion?

DALEK TWO: The drug is to be ta-ken by sec-tions of us, so
            work will not be in-ter-rup-ted.

DALEK ONE: Have you pro-cessed the pic-tures?

DALEK TWO: Ap-pear-ing now on fre-quen-cy six.

            *(The first Dalek operates a control. A
            photograph of the Doctor sitting in the
            jungle clearing appears on the screen.)*

DALEK TWO: It is the el-der pri-son-er.

DALEK ONE: Show se-cond pic-ture.

(The second picture appears. This time it is of SUSAN *and* BARBARA *kneeling beside* ANTODUS *while treating his burns; but the picture has been taken from quite a distance and* ANTODUS *is not in focus.)*

DALEK TWO: The girl and the young wo-man. Is that the body of the fourth pri-son-er, the young man?

DALEK ONE: If so, he has been in-jured.

DALEK TWO: Show third pic-ture.

(This time it is a photograph of IAN *facing* ALYDON.*)*

DALEK TWO: They have made contact with the Thals.

DALEK ONE: It is log-ic-al that to-geth-er they will at-tack us.

3. THE JUNGLE CLEARING (DAY).

*(*IAN *is again facing* ALYDON.*)*

ALYDON: No. And that is my final word.

(He walks away. IAN *stands shaking his head and looking after* ALYDON *before he walks back over to* BARBARA. *Meanwhile,* SUSAN *is amusing herself by climbing in the nearby trees.)*

IAN: Be careful what you're doing up there, Susan.

SUSAN: It's all right, Mr Chesterton. I'm quite safe.

IAN: It's no good. I've tried everything I know. They just won't risk a fight with the Daleks.

(He sits down beside BARBARA.*)*

Trouble is, I can't go too far.

BARBARA: What do you mean?

IAN: Well, why should they help us? Some of them

are bound to get killed. What argument can you use to make a man sacrifice himself for you?

BARBARA: Ian, you don't seem to understand. We'll be prisoners here unless we can think of some way of getting that fluid link back from the Daleks.

IAN: I am quite well aware of that, Barbara.

BARBARA: You know very well they'll find a way out of their city.

IAN: I know.

BARBARA: You know they will.

SUSAN: But they need metal to travel on.

BARBARA: Oh, they'll find a way. They're clever enough. They'll find us and kill us. You know that as well as I do.

IAN: Look, even supposing you're right. I will not ask the Thals to sacrifice themselves for us. I'm sorry, Barbara, I just can't do it.

BARBARA: Ian, why can't you see . . .

(THE DOCTOR *comes out of the TARDIS. He closes the door carefully behind him.* SUSAN *gets up and goes over to him.*)

SUSAN: Any luck, Grandfather?

THE DOCTOR: Hm?

SUSAN: Well, have you made another fluid link yet?

THE DOCTOR: No, I can't, my child. And I've looked through all my spares, and I've really discovered we do need some mercury.

SUSAN: Oh, no!

THE DOCTOR: It puts us in a bit of a jam. I must get that fluid link back again. I'm afraid my little trick has rather rebounded on me . . .

(*He glances over at* IAN.)

Hm . . . what you might call tempting providence, Chesserman.

(IAN _grins at_ THE DOCTOR's _mistake._)

IAN:	Well, don't worry about it now, Doctor, it's happened.
THE DOCTOR:	Yes, well, at least you're not vindictive.
IAN:	Well, I will be if you don't get my name right.
THE DOCTOR:	Hm?
IAN:	It's Chesterton.
THE DOCTOR:	Yes . . . Eh? I know that.
BARBARA:	How can you two stand there wasting time with small talk beats me.
THE DOCTOR:	I can assure you, young lady, I haven't been wasting my time. There's always a way.
SUSAN:	You always think of something, Grandfather.
THE DOCTOR:	Thank you, my dear. Your faith in me is something that I prize very highly. You all realise of course . . . we cannot succeed against the Daleks alone.
BARBARA:	Of course not.
THE DOCTOR:	We have a ready-made army here, the Thals. They're strong and they have one great advantage against the Daleks . . . they can move so much more quickly.
IAN:	Their one great disadvantage . . . they have no arms or ammunition.
THE DOCTOR:	Well, that's all right, young man, the mind will always triumph. With me to lead them, the Thals are bound to succeed!
SUSAN:	But, Grandfather, we've been talking and arguing about this all morning. The Thals won't fight, they're against war.
THE DOCTOR:	My dear child, this is no time for morals. They must fight for us.

IAN:	Why?
THE DOCTOR:	Oh, my dear young man, I do hope you're not going to be difficult.
BARBARA:	The Doctor's right, Ian, can't you see – if only we can get the Thals to attack the city, we could beat the Daleks and get the link back.
THE DOCTOR:	That's just common sense.

(*He peers at* BARBARA.)

	Young lady, I've been underestimating you.
IAN:	I will not allow you to use the Thals to fight for us.
THE DOCTOR:	Are you challenging me?
IAN:	Yes, I am . . .
BARBARA:	Do I have any say in this?
IAN:	Of course you do.
BARBARA:	Well, I think the Doctor's right, and I want to get out of here.
IAN:	I am sorry, I am not having anyone's death on my conscience.
BARBARA:	Except mine . . . and Susan's . . . and the Doctor's.
THE DOCTOR:	Quite so.
IAN:	The only way the Thals can fight is if they themselves want to. It must have nothing whatsoever to do with us.
SUSAN:	I know what you mean. We must help the Thals to save themselves, and not just them help us.
BARBARA:	All you're doing is playing with words.
THE DOCTOR:	We need action, not arguments.
IAN:	Now listen, you two. What victory are you going to show these people when most of them have been killed, eh? A fluid link? Is this what you're going to hold up to them and say 'thank you very much, this is what you fought and died for'?

(*They are all silent.* THE DOCTOR *peers at* IAN *for a moment or two.*)

SUSAN: The thing is, can the Thals still fight?

IAN: Well, that's what we've got to find out. Are they cowards, or are they just against fighting on principle?

BARBARA: Well, how can we find out?

IAN: Well, I've got an idea, but whatever I do, don't interfere . . . I'm not even sure that I'm right.

(*He goes over to the Thals' history capsule.*)

Well . . . let's see what happens.

THE DOCTOR: Hm. Strange young man.

SUSAN: He's right, though.

BARBARA: Yes, he is.

THE DOCTOR: Yes, we'll see.

(*In another part of the clearing,* IAN *is talking to* ALYDON. *Other Thals gradually gather round to listen.*)

IAN: . . . to have self-respect. At this moment anyone could come in here. They could rob, they could steal . . .

THE DOCTOR: Let's see what he's up to.

IAN: . . . they could even kill you. And you wouldn't lift a finger to help yourselves.

ALYDON: We will not fight. There will be no more wars. Look at our planet! This was once a great world, full of ideas and art and invention. In one day it was destroyed, and you'll never find one good reason why we should ever begin destroying everything again.

(THE DOCTOR *looks at* BARBARA, *gestures hopelessly and turns away.*)

I'm sorry.

IAN: You're not sorry! You stand here mumbling a
                lot of words out of your history, but it means
                nothing. Nothing at all!

                (ALYDON *accepts this with a faint shrug.*
                Try as he might, IAN *cannot provoke*
                anger in him. Suddenly, he remembers the
                history capsule.)

                You carry this around with you . . . your history
                records. Well, it must be valuable to you.
                Supposing I take it down to the city and try and
                trade with the Daleks, eh? Perhaps they'd think
                it valuable enough to exchange for our fluid link.

                (ALYDON *makes a move towards* IAN *and*
                then checks himself.)

ALYDON: I don't believe you'd do it.
IAN: I would.

ALYDON: None of us would stop you.

                (IAN *looks around him.* DYONI *is standing*
                close by. He has an idea.)

IAN: If I don't get the link back, the four of us will
                die. Perhaps the Daleks are more interested in
                people. Maybe they were holding us to
                experiment on us. I could take them an
                alternative.

                (*He goes over to* DYONI, *seizes her by the*
                wrist and starts to move. BARBARA *moves*
                to intervene but THE DOCTOR *stops her. He*
                realises what IAN *is trying to do.* IAN *moves*
                a few steps further. DYONI *moves with*
                him, bewildered. ALYDON *moves quickly,*
                takes IAN *by the shoulder and hits him,*

knocking him to the ground. IAN *rubs his chin ruefully.*)

So there is something you'll fight for!

4. A CORRIDOR.

(*A Dalek weaves wildly about, it's eye-, gun- and sucker-sticks jerking crazily.*)

DALEK: Help! Can-not con-trol. Can-not con-trol. Help me. Help me. Help. Help. Help. Help. Aaargh! Aaargh! Aaargh! Aaaaaargh!! . . .

5. THE DALEK CONTROL ROOM.

(*Two Daleks are by the control console. A light flashes and a voice sounds over the intercom.*)

DALEK: (*OOV*) Em-erg-en-cy! Em-er-gen-cy! All Dal-eks in sec-tion three are in-cap-ab-le of work-ing.

DALEK TWO: Sec-tion three? That was the first sec-tion to get the an-ti ra-di-at-ion drug re-ceived from the Thals.

DALEK ONE: Stand by for a gen-er-al an-nounce-ment.

(*He operates a control.*)

This is con-trol. All dis-trib-ut-ion of the an-ti ra-di-at-ion drug is to be stopped im-med-iate-ly!

(*He turns off the microphone control.*)

The Da-lek race has become con-dit-ioned to ra-di-at-ion.

DALEK TWO: But if you are right, we are in dan-ger.

DALEK: (*OOV*) All Da-leks in sec-tion three are dy-ing.

DALEK ONE:	They must be ex-am-ined im-med-i-at-ely.
DALEK TWO:	Look! The di-sease has reached us in here.

> (*Another Dalek in the room has started to go out of control.*)

DALEK ONE:	Then we can-not de-lay.
DALEK TWO:	But what are we to do? Is this the end of the Da-leks?
DALEK ONE:	We need ra-di-at-ion to sur-vive. So we must in-crease our sup-ply of ra-di-at-ion.
DALEK TWO:	But there is only one way to do that.
DALEK ONE:	Ex-act-ly. We may have to ex-plode an-oth-er neu-tron bomb.

6. *THE JUNGLE CLEARING* (*NIGHT*).

> (*Most of the Thals are sleeping. Here and there are some flickering lamps.* DYONI *is still awake.* ALYDON *also cannot sleep.* DYONI *comes over to him and kneels down beside him.*)

DYONI:	Why don't you sleep?
ALYDON:	Presently.
DYONI:	Are you angry with yourself for striking the young man?
ALYDON:	No, I . . . I knew he was trying to make me do it . . . I still couldn't stop myself . . . Do you despise me for hitting him?
DYONI:	If you hadn't fought him, I think I would have hated you.
ALYDON:	I knew he wouldn't really take you and give you to the Daleks. But I fought him. I wish Temmosus were here. What would he have said, Dyoni? Which is the most important? To . . . to . . . fight and live . . . or to die without fighting?

(BARBARA *and* GANATUS *have been listening to the conversation, and now move away.*)

7. *THE OTHER SIDE OF THE CLEARING.*

(BARBARA *and* GANATUS *sit down on his cloak.*)

BARBARA: What will happen now?

GANATUS: I don't know. We always do what the leader of our race decides for us. He never decides anything without our full approval.

BARBARA: And if Alydon decides not to help us?

(GANATUS *is silent.*)

Well, we'll have to wait till the morning . . .

(*She returns to gazing off into the distance.*)

What's that light in the sky? It's a reflection from the city, I suppose.

GANATUS: No, the lake. Some sort of chemical in the water that makes it glow in the moonlight.

BARBARA: You've been down there?

GANATUS: Yes. There's horror down there in the swamp. Five of us went there in search of food and . . . only my brother and I came back.

BARBARA: Well, what happened to the others?

GANATUS: We found what was left of . . . one of them. The lake is alive with mutations, bred and cross-bred until the original has long been replaced by . . .

(*He stops.*)

I'm sorry, I'm being morbid.

BARBARA: Oh, I don't mind as long as we're this far away. But I wonder the Daleks haven't cleaned it out – killed everything.

GANATUS: Why should they? Isn't that the perfect defence for the back of the city? Only a fool would attack the city from the lake.

8. *THE DALEK CONTROL ROOM.*

(*Two Daleks are in the room.*)

DALEK ONE: Has the an-ti ra-di-at-ion drug dis-trib-ut-ion been stopped?

DALEK TWO: Yes. On-ly Da-leks in sec-tion two and three re-ceived it. All Da-leks in sec-tion three have now died.

(*The first Dalek operates a control.*)

DALEK ONE: Da-leks in sec-tion two are to be brought to the So-nic Cham-ber.

(*He turns off the intercom.*)

DALEK TWO: We will di-rect the air pol-lut-ed by ra-di-at-ion away from the nu-cle-ar re-ac-tors into the So-nic Cham-ber.

DALEK ONE: And if they do not die . . . . we shall have our ans-wer.

DALEK TWO: But if we need ra-di-at-ion, we can ne-ver re-build the world out-side.

DALEK ONE: We do not have to a-dapt to the en-vir-on-ment. We will change the en-vir-on-ment to suit us.

9. *THE JUNGLE CLEARING* (*DAY*).

(THE DOCTOR, SUSAN, IAN *and* BARBARA *are together in a group. The Thals, headed by* DYONI *and* GANATUS *, are also together, facing them.* ALYDON *now comes to the front of his group.*)

ALYDON: I have one question to ask of you. If we do not help you, what will you do?

IAN: We'll find our way into the city and take back our lost equipment.

(ALYDON *nods and turns to face his people.*)

ALYDON: You see, we cannot stand by and let these people die. If we do not help them it would be the same as if we'd killed them ourselves. The way I have reasoned is this. The Daleks are strong and they hate us. And I am sure they will find a way to come out of their city and kill us. So it is not merely a question of whether we go off in a vain search for food, and in all probability starve to death. We face death now. In the city is enough food for all of us and all of the Daleks, a hundred times over. My conclusion is this. There is no indignity in being afraid to die. But there is a terrible shame in being afraid to live. If none of you agree with my reasons, then let me go with these people and I will help you elect a new chief.

(*There is a moment's silence.*)

GANATUS: I'll go with you, Alydon.

ELYON: And I.

KRISTAS: Let's start at once!

ANTODUS: And I.

(*The Thals echo their agreement.*)

IAN: Thank you.

(GANATUS *steps forward, holding a map of the city.* ALYDON *looks at him.*)

ALYDON: You knew what my decision would be?

GANATUS: I could always have destroyed it if you'd decided differently.

(*They smile at each other.*)

THE DOCTOR: If we get this intelligent anticipation, we shall succeed. Let us see this. Now, what is this area here?

GANATUS: The swamp. Here are the mountains, this is the far side of the city. I've been into the swamp, its surrounded by lakes here, do you see? The lakes are inhabited by all sorts of strange creatures.

IAN: Can we get into the city this way.

ALYDON: Over the mountains?

IAN: Yes.

GANATUS: That means going through that swamp.

ALYDON: We can't go through the swamp – it's too dangerous.

GANATUS: It is dangerous, yes, but I realised last night when I was talking to Barbara that it is undefended.

ALYDON: Undefended? It's a perfect natural barrier, all those creatures . . . you know that yourself.

GANATUS: Yes, I know, but I mean the Daleks won't be on guard there. There's a chance to take them by surprise. Believe me, I'm not happy about this, but it's the best possible chance there is.

THE DOCTOR: Yes, yes, well now, I suggest we split into two groups. The one to distract the Daleks on the city wall side, and the other to try and force a way through the mountains.

IAN: Yes, I think that's the best plan.

THE DOCTOR: Are we all agreed?

(*There is a murmour of approval from the crowd.*)

ALYDON: Yes, very well, then . . . that is what we must do.

> _10. THE DALEK CONTROL ROOM._
>
> (_There is an intermittent buzzing sound. The two Daleks present turn towards a scanner screen. One of them turns a dial._)

DALEK ONE: The La-ser-scope is trans-mit-ting. The qua-li-ty is poor.

> (_The image on the screen keeps breaking up,_ IAN, BARBARA _and a small group of Thals can just about be made out, moving towards the city._)

What has hap-pened? Has this group bro-ken a-way? Is there a plan be-hind it? Why di-vide their forc-es?

> (_A ticker-tape type machine starts to churn out tape nearby, and the other Dalek turns to examine it._)

DALEK TWO: The fi-gures are com-ing through on the ra-di-at-ion treat-ment.

DALEK ONE: Dis-con-tin-ue la-ser-scope.

> (_The scanner goes blank._)

DALEK TWO: There is an im-prove-ment. Ex-cept for one ser-ious case, all Da-leks in sect-ion two have shown signs of re-cov-ery.

DALEK ONE: Then our po-sit-ion is clear. For us the drug is a poi-son.

DALEK TWO: And ra-di-at-ion is still nec-ess-ary to us.

DALEK ONE: Es-sent-ial.

> (_He turns on the intercom._)

I want a com-plete sur-vey on our stock of nuc-lear mat-er-ials. I want an es-ti-mate of the a-mount of waste mat-ter from the nuc-le-ar re-ac-tors.

11. THE SWAMP (NIGHT).

(*A dense mist hangs eerily over the water. Occasional bubbles of gas break on its surface.* GANATUS *appears and looks suspiciously at the swamp.* ANTODUS *is by his side.*)

ANTODUS:	We'll never get through!
GANATUS:	Yes, we will.
ANTODUS:	What makes you think it'll be any different to the first time?
GANATUS:	At least we know what to expect.
ANTODUS:	But the others don't.
GANATUS:	We promised Alydon we'd find a way through the mountains, and that's what we're going to do.
ANTODUS:	You'd never get the others to follow you if you told them what happened the first time. It's your duty to tell them. How we watched Amezus dragged beneath the waters of the lake. How you and I ran in terror when . . .
GANATUS:	That's enough! We're going on, Antodus. You keep your fears to yourself. I don't want you upsetting the others, is that clear?

(ANTODUS *mumbles half-heartedly.*)

ANTODUS:	Yes . . .
GANATUS:	Well, is it?
ANTODUS:	Yes!

(ANTODUS *pulls away.* GANATUS *stares at*

the mist rising from the swamp. IAN *joins him, followed by* BARBARA *and the rest of the group.*)

GANATUS: Well, this is the swamp. From now on, it's going to be rather uncomfortable.

IAN: Yes, I see what you mean.

GANATUS: The ground's very uneven – sometimes rock, sometimes thick mud. You'll have to watch how you walk. I think it'll be a wise plan to find a place to rest for the night.

IAN: Yes, well, we've made very good time.

(*He looks at his watch.*)

It's only taken us four hours to get here from the edge of the forest. That leaves us with two-and-a-half days to go through the mountains to the city.

GANATUS: If there is a way through.

IAN: We'll find a way.

(GANATUS *glances at Ian with a slight smile.*)

I'll go and give Barbara a hand.

GANATUS: I'm surprised you let her come.

IAN: I'd have been more surprised if I could have stopped her.

(GANATUS *smiles and moves off. The Thals move past and, when* BARBARA *gets close he puts out a hand and takes her arm.*)

How are you doing?

BARBARA: Fine . . . Oh, I'm glad the mountaineering's over.

IAN: There'll be some more, once we get through this little lot.

BARBARA: We're going through there?

(She looks at the swamp in horror and disgust.)

IAN: Well, we must. We've got a deadline with the Doctor in two-and-a-half days, and we've got to make it.

BARBARA: Well, I think we could all do with a rest.

IAN: No, we'll keep up with the others. They'll be breaking camp soon.

(BARBARA resigns herself and follows on.)

Now take care – watch where you put your feet. All right?

BARBARA: Yes.

12. NEARBY THE SWAMP'S EDGE.

(Something raises its head from the water and BARBARA gasps. IAN hits at it with a stick. They move on.)

GANATUS: This looks like a fairly dry section.

IAN: Yes, it'll do.

GANATUS: Right, we'll make camp here.

(He issues instructions to some of the other Thals.)

Gather up some dry branches. It'll make it more comfortable to sleep on.

(The others move to obey. BARBARA spreads a cloak on the ground and sinks gratefully down on to it.)

Barbara, you see to the food, I'll get the fire going.

BARBARA: Right.

GANATUS: At least it might stop some of these . . . these things from bothering us.

> *13. THE LAKESIDE.*
>
> (*There is a small pool.* IAN *cups his hands and splashes water over his face.*)
>
> *14. THE SWAMP.*
>
> (BARBARA *and the Thals are sitting round a flickering lamp. Suddenly they freeze as a primeval roar echoes through the air.*)
>
> *15. THE LAKESIDE.*
>
> (IAN *jumps up in terror as a huge octopus-like creature starts to rise up out of the swamp directly in front of him. As it rises, two enormous eyes light up. Ian runs back to the others.*)
>
> *16. THE SWAMP.*

BARBARA: What was it? Did you see anything?

IAN: Yes it was a . . .

GANATUS: Kristas, stand guard here, will you?

KRISTAS: Right.

GANATUS: We'll take the first watch between us.

> (GANATUS *shepherds the others further back away from the lake edge.*)

IAN: I'm all right, really, I . . .

GANATUS: Yes, I know that, but I think you two Earth people should get as much sleep as possible. We're more used to this kind of life. It's over a

year since we left our own plateau in search of a
new source of food. I've almost forgotten what it
was like to stay in one place and enjoy it . . . I
suppose there'll be an end to it one day.

17. THE SWAMP (DAWN).

(*A hand shakes* IAN *and he starts up. It is*
GANATUS. *He smiles at* IAN.)

GANATUS: It's time to move, my friend.

IAN: You let me sleep.

GANATUS: Yes.

IAN: Why didn't you wake me?

(*Before he can reply,* ELYON *appears and
comes over to* GANATUS.)

ELYON: Ganatus . . .

GANATUS: What's the matter?

ELYON: Come and see what I've found by the lake.

GANATUS: Right.

IAN: Hold on, I'll come with you.

(IAN *starts to get up out of his makeshift
bed. As he does,* BARBARA – *lying beside
him – is just waking.*)

Morning.

BARBARA: Morning . . . Oh, for a feather pillow and a
spring mattress.

(*She rubs her neck gingerly.*)

18. THE LAKESIDE.

(ELYON *is standing. There are several
water-bags at his feet.*)

GANATUS: What did you see?

ELYON: Over there . . .

(He points to a series of pipes that can be seen emerging from a cliff face and running on down into the lake.)

IAN: We were right. The Daleks do get their water from the lake.

GANATUS: But how do we get to the city from there?

IAN: Well, there must be a way. I mean, the Daleks aren't very mobile. They must have cut a pathway through there to work on the pipeline.

GANATUS: How long do you think it'll take us to reach them?

ELYON: Most of today. If we could cross the lake, we could reach it much quicker.

IAN: I'm sorry, that's one way I'm not going!

ELYON: Well, it would be dangerous, certainly. The lake is full of mutations, but . . .

GANATUS: No, we must go round.

IAN: Yes, and we ought to try and get there before the sun goes down.

ELYON: Well, I'll just go and fill the water-bags.

(GANATUS nods. ELYON draws him aside.)

There's no point in trying to cross the lake, you think?

GANATUS: No, no, he's right. Anyway, think of how long it would take to build a raft.

(He rejoins IAN and they move away, leaving ELYON to fill the water-bags.)

19. THE SWAMP.

(BARBARA is handing round cups of a steaming-hot liquid.)

IAN:	Barbara, we saw some pipes going into the lake.
BARBARA:	So we can go through?
IAN:	Well, maybe with a bit of luck, eh?

(BARBARA *hands him a cup.*)

Thanks. Hm . . . good.

BARBARA:	Where's Elyon?
GANATUS:	He's gone to fill the water-bags. He won't be long.

20. THE LAKESIDE.

(ELYON *bends down and starts to fill the water-bags. Suddenly the water starts to bubble and boil.* ELYON *turns as a whirlpool starts to form in the water directly in front of him.*)

21. THE SWAMP.

(*Without warning, a terrible, human scream echoes around them.* IAN *and* GANATUS *leap to their feet.*)

GANATUS: Stay here!

(*They run off towards the lake.*)

Next Episode:
THE ORDEAL

EPISODE SIX

THE ORDEAL

1. THE LAKESIDE.

(ELYON *bends down and starts to fill the water-bags. Suddenly the water starts to bubble and boil.* ELYON *turns as a whirlpool forms in the water directly in front of him.*)

2. THE SWAMP.

(*Without warning, a terrible human scream echoes around them.* IAN *and* GANATUS *leap to their feet.*)

GANATUS: Stay here!

(*They run off towards the lake.*)

3. THE LAKESIDE.

(IAN, GANATUS, BARBARA *and* KRISTAS *arrive. They stare helplessly around* IAN *picks up one of the water-bags. He looks towards the lake, where several other water-bags are floating on the surface as the whirlpool gradually subsides.* ANTODUS *runs up to the others.*)

ANTODUS: What is it? What's happened to Elyon?

(*There is a pause, each of them waiting for someone else to pass on the terrible news.*)

IAN: There's nothing we can do here.

BARBARA: Ian . . .

(IAN *leads her away.* KRISTAS *follows.*)

ANTODUS: Did . . . Elyon . . . fall in? What happened?

(ANTODUS *bends down and examines one of the water-bags.* GANATUS *tries to reassure him.*)

GANATUS: It must have happened very quickly. Come on now, we must reach the cliffs by tonight.

(*Taking one last look at the lake, they leave.*)

4. *A RIDGE IN THE JUNGLE.*

(SUSAN *is looking through* THE DOCTOR*'s binocular glasses. She goes back over to a rock, behind which* THE DOCTOR, ALYDON *and* DYONI *are crouching. She hands the glasses to* ALYDON. THE DOCTOR *is studying some sort of map and* SUSAN *indicates the features of the city that she has just seen.*)

SUSAN: There are four roads that lead up from the main square, going North, South, East and West.

(DYONI *draws in the roads.* ALYDON *stares into the distance at the city with the binoculars.*)

ALYDON: The main ventilators seem to be over in this section.

(ALYDON *indicates a place on the map.*)

THE DOCTOR: Mmm . . .

SUSAN: Oh, that's right. It goes down there, and up.

THE DOCTOR: Can you see any way in at all?

ALYDON: No.

THE DOCTOR: Then allow me, will you?

> (*He takes the glasses from* ALYDON *and stands up from behind the rock.*)

SUSAN: Grandfather, get down!

THE DOCTOR: Yes, yes, yes. Now the . . . the things we have to put out of action are the radio and television waves. They've obviously got complete coverage in and around the city.

ALYDON: They don't leave much to chance.

THE DOCTOR: We must presume they don't leave anything to chance.

DYONI: But if they have pictures of the entrance to the city, how can we do anything.

THE DOCTOR: Then we must stop the pictures. Remember, the Daleks aren't very mobile.

SUSAN: Yes, we do have speed on our side.

THE DOCTOR: And there's always value in surprise. I know it looks difficult, but we must try it, my friends. Yes, we must!

ALYDON: Yes. I wish I knew what they were planning for us.

5. *THE DALEK CONTROL ROOM.*

DALEK ONE: The re-port for the neu-tron bomb is pre-pared.

DALEK TWO: Let us hear it.

> (*The first Dalek operates a control.*)

DALEK: (*OOV*) Re-port on neu-tron bomb. To co-ver
            five hun-dred square miles, time to con-struct,
            twen-ty-three days.

DALEK ONE: Is that the short-est pos-sible time?

DALEK: (*OOV*) Yes.

DALEK ONE: Ve-ry well.

    (*The Dalek turns off the intercom.*)

It is too long.

DALEK TWO: We must a-ban-don the i-de-a of a neu-tron
            bomb.

DALEK ONE: We must find a-noth-er way of spread-ing ra-dia-
            tion.

    6. *A Cave* (*Night*).

    (GANATUS *leads the way, holding a torch
to illuminate the path.* BARBARA *is close
behind him. She stumbles, but manages to
recover.*)

GANATUS: It's getting narrower.

BARBARA: Oh, it's like all the other caves . . . just tails off
            into a dead end.

GANATUS: There's a gloomy thought for you.

BARBARA: I wonder if Ian is doing any better?

GANATUS: When did we arrange to meet him and the
            others?

BARBARA: Oh, we ought to be going back now.

GANATUS: . . . make sure this is impossible first.

    (*He suddenly stops, as the cave appears to
come to a dead end.*)

Huh! I must have a sixth sense. Look at that . . .
pity. Well, let's go back and try one of the other
ways.

BARBARA: No, wait a minute.

GANATUS: Can you see something?

BARBARA: No . . . stand still for a minute.

(*They both stand motionless and silent.*)

There! Can you hear it? The sound of water!

(GANATUS *plays the beam of his torch over the overhanging rocks. Suddenly the beam picks up a narrow opening several feet from the ground.*)

GANATUS: Yes . . . Yes, Barbara, look! There's a passageway here.

BARBARA: Well, that won't be easy.

GANATUS: It's a good job we haven't been over-eating recently. It's going to be a long crawl.

(*He shines his torch through the narrow opening.*)

Well, we won't use one of the customs of your planet.

BARBARA: What's that?

GANATUS: Ladies first!

BARBARA: Ha! I should hope not.

(GANATUS *ties the rope he is carrying to his belt.*)

GANATUS: Pay the rope out as I move in, will you?

BARBARA: Yes, all right. Be careful. Remember what Ian said – we're not to take any chances.

GANATUS: Do you always do what Ian says?

BARBARA: No, I don't.

GANATUS: Well, let me have the torch, then. Unless you think . . .

BARBARA: No, no, your need is greater than mine.

            (BARBARA *picks up the rope and starts to pay it out.*)

GANATUS: (*OOV*) Barbara?

BARBARA: Yes?

7. THE EDGE OF A CLIFF.

GANATUS: There seems to be a drop of about thirty feet or so . . . I'm going down.

8. THE CAVE.

BARBARA: Well, be careful!

GANATUS: (*OOV*) Tie your end of the rope around a rock or something, will you?

BARBARA: Yes, all right.

            (BARBARA *winds the rope around a large boulder several times, and holds on tightly to the end.*)

            Ready!

            (*The slack rope snakes off down the passageway.*)

GANATUS: (*OOV*) Right!

            (*As the full weight of* GANATUS *is felt, the rope begins to slip.* BARBARA *tries desperately to hold on.*)

9. THE CLIFF-FACE.

            (GANATUS *is hanging half-way down the face of the cliff, suspended by the rope.*)

10. THE CAVE.

(BARBARA *tries to stop the rope slipping further but the weight is too much for her. She slips and the rope snakes out through the narrow opening.*)

11. THE BOTTOM OF THE CLIFF.

(GANATUS *lands heavily on the rock floor at the base of the cliff and lies motionless.*)

12. THE CAVE.

BARBARA: Ganatus! Ganatus!

(BARBARA *turns to run for help, but runs straight into* IAN.)

IAN: What's happened?

BARBARA: I couldn't hold on to it.

IAN: Where's Ganatus?

BARBARA: It slipped through my fingers. He's down here, look!

13. THE BOTTOM OF THE CLIFF.

GANATUS: Barbara?

IAN: (*OOV*) All right this end. Are you hurt?

GANATUS: No, I'm not.

14. THE CAVE.

(ANTODUS *runs into view.*)

ANTODUS: Is my brother hurt?

BARBARA: No, he isn't, but it was my fault. The rope slipped off the rock.

IAN: The rope, Antodus!

(ANTODUS *takes his coil of rope and they lower it down.*)

15. *THE BOTTOM OF THE CLIFF.*

GANATUS: Barbara?

16. *THE EDGE OF THE CLIFF.*

IAN: Are you sure you're all right?

17. *THE BOTTOM OF THE CLIFF.*

GENATUS: Yes. What's happened to Barbara?

18. *THE EDGE OF THE CLIFF.*

IAN: She's OK. Don't worry. Hang on a minute. I'm bringing another rope down to you.

(IAN *is tying the rope around his waist.*)

19. *THE BOTTOM OF THE CLIFF.*

GANATUS: It would be better if you came down here. There's a big cavern with lots of tunnels going off it. Unless you've found anything else, this seems a fair chance.

IAN: (*OOV*) No, we haven't. Hang on, we'll be with you in a couple of minutes.

GANATUS: Good! It looks as though it may have been a lucky fall.

20. *THE DALEK CONTROL ROOM.*

(*One of the two Daleks in the room operates the intercom.*)

DALEK: (*OOV*) Ran-ger-scopes are re-cord-ing great act-iv-it-y a-mongst the Thal peo-ple.

DALEK ONE: Are there pic-tures?

DALEK: (*OOV*) No. Re-cept-ion is bad.

(*The Dalek switches off the intercom.*)

DALEK ONE: They are at-tack-ing our in-stru-ments.

DALEK TWO: We must keep a-lert.

DALEK ONE: Yes. Con-centrate all pow-er of ran-ger-scopes and vi-bro-scopes on all ent-ran-ces to the ci-ty.

21. A RIDGE IN THE JUNGLE (EVENING).

(DYONI *and other Thals are aiming mirrors at the antennae on the Daleks' city, in an attempt to blind them.*)

22. THE CITY WALL.

THE DOCTOR: It looks as if my plan has worked.

ALYDON: We can't keep up this light reflection for long.

THE DOCTOR: Never mind. It gives us a better chance to get into the city unnoticed.

SUSAN: You can't be sure of that, Grandfather.

THE DOCTOR: Oh, I know it's risky, but er . . . well, we mustn't diddle about here, now . . . I want to get to the east side of that antenna.

ALYDON: Doctor, look!

THE DOCTOR: Mm?

ALYDON: According to the map, we should be moving further to our left, in that direction.

SUSAN: Yes.

THE DOCTOR: Yes, yes, I see. Well you go ahead, will you? Go along, child . . . yes, we'll show them a thing or two.

23. A TUNNEL IN THE CAVE.

IAN: So far, so good! It seems to be broadening out a bit.

GANATUS:	Who knows? It may stop being impossible.
BARBARA:	Just become unbearable.
IAN:	Well, at least we can breathe in here.
GANATUS:	We seem to be travelling more or less in a straight line.
IAN:	Yes, I think we are.
KRISTAS:	I'll take the fire for a bit.
IAN:	Oh, thank you.
KRISTAS:	Shall I lead on, then?
IAN:	Yes, I suppose you might as well. We'll . . . we'll have a rest in a minute.

(KRISTAS *moves off with the torch,* IAN *and* BARBARA *follow.* GANATUS *waits for his brother,* ANTODUS, *to join the others, but he hestitates and grips* GANATUS's *arm.*)

ANTODUS:	Ganatus . . . I want to go back.
GANATUS:	What for?
ANTODUS:	I can't go on any more.
GANATUS:	You must!
ANTODUS:	No. We're going deeper . . . deeper all the time. We'll be trapped in the mountain, I know we will. Please, Ganatus, let me go back.
GANATUS:	You can't!
ANTODUS:	But you don't really need me, not really. I could . . . well, I could go back and signal to the others that we've managed to get as far as we have.
GANATUS:	Antodus! We go on together!
ANTODUS:	Why? Why are you making me do all these things? Even if we do get through, we'll never defeat the Daleks . . . Ganatus, we're all going to be killed!
GANATUS:	We can't turn back now.
ANTODUS:	The others can't . . . but we could. Listen,

they're going to die anyway. We could just go back and tell the others that the Daleks killed them.

GANATUS: Oh, what are you talking about? You mustn't go back!

ANTODUS: I'm not going on.

GANATUS: You are . . . you must!

(ANTODUS *tries to back away, but* GANATUS *seizes his arm. They struggle and* GANATUS *lashes out at his brother.*)

Antodus, I'm sorry, are . . . are you hurt?

(*Suddenly there is a cracking sound from above.*)

Ian!

(*The roof starts to fall in on them. Desperately* GANATUS *drags his brother further down into the cave, in the direction of the others. A cloud of dust billows after them.*)

IAN: Is he hurt?

GANATUS: A rock hit him. It would have hit me but . . . he pushed me aside. He was very brave.

IAN: Well, I hope he hasn't cut his head.

(*He starts to examine* ANTODUS's *head but* ANTODUS *pulls away.*)

ANTODUS: I'm all right.

(IAN *senses something is going on. He looks from one brother to the other, but can't work it out.*)

GANATUS: Ian, we can't go back the way we came. We must go on now.

> (*As he is speaking,* GANATUS *is looking down at his brother, for whom this speech is intended.*)

24. THE DALEK CONTROL ROOM.

DALEK ONE: E-merg-enc-y! E-merg-enc-y!

DALEK TWO: Re-act-ion on the vib-ra-scopes.

DALEK ONE: Where?

DALEK TWO: Sec-tion fif-teen. City wall. Shall I re-direct the ran-ger-scopes?

DALEK ONE: No. If we track them by their vib-rat-ions we can take them by sur-prise.

25. THE CITY WALL.

> (*On the wall a few feet from the ground is a small box, with a front panel made of glass. Inside there are various terminals and wires and a number of glass rods. A single, larger wire runs out of the box and along the wall.*)

SUSAN: Hey, Grandfather. Look!

THE DOCTOR: Mm? . . . Yes?

SUSAN: Is this what you want?

THE DOCTOR: Ah yes, a single cable. The whole city is powered by static electricity.

ALYDON: Well, how do you know that?

THE DOCTOR: The single wire you see. Round here . . . there. See? And there? That must be the answer.

> (ALYDON *obviously does not see.*)

SUSAN: Well, it leads up to the antennae.

ALYDON: Well, it certainly goes in that direction. I . . . I can't see it all.

SUSAN: I wonder if I can open this box?

THE DOCTOR: Hm?

SUSAN: There aren't any hinges on it.

(*She examines it further.*)

Well, that's it – look . . . look, it slides up!

THE DOCTOR: Ah, good girl! Now just take it over there. That's it. Now look out!

(*He smashes the glass rods inside the control box, laughing as he does so.*)

SUSAN: The thing is, how are we going to cut the wire now that it's exposed, without getting a terrific shock?

ALYDON: Look, we can't wait around here too long, you know.

THE DOCTOR: No, just a minute. Now you go and tell your friends to stop flashing the light on the antennae. Because for all we know, the Daleks might have a beam to throw on them . . . paralyse them . . . kill them.

ALYDON: But I can't leave you two here.

THE DOCTOR: Oh, we shall be all right. Now go along and tell them to move their position from time to time. Now, hurry, please.

ALYDON: Very well then, but don't waste time here. I'll come back for you if I can.

THE DOCTOR: Yes, yes, yes, yes. We shall be back before then. Now go. Dear, dear, dear, that young man gets so agitated. Now I'll tell you what we'll do, we'll short-circuit it to . . . another conductor. Let me have the key of the Ship, Susan, will you?

SUSAN: Hm?

THE DOCTOR: The key of the Ship, dear.

SUSAN: Oh, what a good idea! Yes.

THE DOCTOR: Yes, yes, yes! I can always make another one . . . if necessary.

SUSAN: Yes, of course.

THE DOCTOR: Now let us er . . . proceed.

> (*He holds the key-chain on the end of his walking stick and pushes it into the heart of the control box.*)

THE DOCTOR: Now, the power's running away. That'll teach the Daleks to meddle in our affairs.

SUSAN: What about this one?

> (SUSAN *indicates another, smaller box just above the main one.*)

THE DOCTOR: Well, of course!

> (*He smashes the glass casing and picks up the dangling end of the key-chain, using his walking stick, and then connects it to the other control box. There is a blinding flash.*)

> 25. *THE DALEK CONTROL ROOM.*

> (*A section of the control panel short-circuits, and there is another flash of light.*)

> 27. *THE CITY WALL.*

THE DOCTOR: Now . . . we've . . . we've shorted it, you see. So something must have gone somewhere else. The extent of the damage of course we don't know yet.

SUSAN: Look, Grandfather, this is marvellous, but . . .

but they must have a fault locator somewhere. We must get away from here.

THE DOCTOR: But, my dear child, don't you realise what I've done? A few simple tools . . .

SUSAN: Yes, but we must . . .

THE DOCTOR: A superior brain . . .

(SUSAN *gasps, and as* THE DOCTOR *turns several Daleks move to surround them.*)

28. *THE EDGE OF THE RAVINE.*

(IAN *moves forward, leading the group, and then abruptly stops.*)

IAN: Look out!

(*The others cluster behind him.*)

No place for a quiet stroll, is it?

(IAN *shines the torch downwards and the edge of a chasm looms before them.*)

GANATUS: It looks pretty wide.

IAN: Yes . . . and deep. Well, you might as well take a rest while we sort this one out.

(BARBARA, KRISTAS *and* ANTODUS *sink to the floor, exhausted.* GANATUS *and* IAN *crouch at the edge, playing the flashlight on the far side of the chasm.*)

IAN: No point in going that way – it widens out. There's no foothold at all on this side. There's a ledge over there, look, about two to three feet, would you say?

GANATUS: Hm . . . There seems to be some sort of cleft in the rock-face . . . there.

IAN:	Yes, I think you're right. We'll have to get over there.
GANATUS:	How about . . . going down this side on a rope, then trying to climb the other?
IAN:	Yes, well, see how deep it is. Hold the torch . . . a pebble . . .

(IAN *picks up a small stone from the floor and tosses it down into the chasm. They both wait, and after what seems like an eternity there is a faint sound of a splash from far below.*)

GANATUS:	How do we do it?
IAN:	We jump.

(GANATUS *looks doubtfully across at the narrow ledge on the other side of the chasm.*)

GANATUS:	There's not much space to land in.
IAN:	No.
GANATUS:	Oh, well . . . I'll go . . .
IAN:	You go and tell them we're going to jump.

(GANATUS *goes back to the others.*)

GANATUS:	We're going to jump it.

(IAN *takes the end of the rope and fixes it around his waist.*)

IAN:	Shine the torch on that ledge. Keep clear of me when I run, and give me plenty of rope.

(GANATUS *and the others take hold of the rope.*)

BARBARA:	Good luck!

(IAN *moves back down the passageway
and measures the rope needed before he
runs towards the chasm. He takes a flying
leap and lands heavily against the wall on
the far side of the ledge.*)

IAN: All right . . . Ganatus, you come over next, and
we'll explore that cleft in the rock.

GANATUS: Right. Quite firm?

IAN: I think there's just about enough room for two
of us.

GANATUS: Take up the slack, will you?

IAN: Right!

BARBARA: Good luck!

(GANATUS *smiles at her, then looks across
towards* IAN.)

GANATUS: Ready?

IAN: Right . . . take a good long run!

(GANATUS *moves back, runs forward and
also successfully lands on the far side.* IAN
*grabs hold of him to steady him. He gets
to his feet.*)

Good jump! You should have come first.

(GANATUS *unties the rope from his waist.*)

GANATUS: Now, I'll take a look at this cleft . . . The torch?

(*One of the others throws it across to him.
He moves off down the ledge, which
narrows further on. He spreadeagles himself against the rock-face.*)

Pay it out slowly.

IAN: Right!

GANATUS: It's all right, there's . . . a handhold just here.

(*He rounds a bend and disappears from view.*)

GANATUS: A little more rope . . . It goes wider. It seems to be some sort of a tunnel. I . . . I don't need the rope any more. Bring the others over.

IAN: Right . . . rope coming over!

29. THE DALEK CONTROL ROOM.

(THE DOCTOR *and* SUSAN *are sitting together on the floor in the pool of light. Daleks surround them.*)

DALEK ONE: You have dest-royed our vid-e-o-scope and one of our lifts.

THE DOCTOR: And you in turn killed the Thal leader in your ambush. You will be responsible for more deaths unless you help these people.

DALEK ONE: The on-ly in-ter-est we have in the Thals is their to-tal ex-term-in-at-ion.

SUSAN: What do you mean?

DALEK ONE: To-mor-row the at-mos-phere will be bom-bard-ed by the ra-dia-tion from our nuc-le-ar re-act-ors.

SUSAN: Why are you doing this?

THE DOCTOR: That's sheer murder.

DALEK ONE: No. Ex-ter-min-at-ion.

THE DOCTOR: But you must listen to reason. Please, you must!

DALEK ONE: With-out ra-di-a-tion, the Da-lek race is end-ed. We need it as you and the Thals need air.

(*All the Daleks suddenly join in unison in a deafening chorus.*)

DALEKS: To-mor-row we will be the mas-ters of the pla-net Ska-ro!

30. THE EDGE OF THE RAVINE.

(BARBARA *jumps across the chasm.* IAN *catches her as she lands.*)

BARBARA: Oh, I thought I . . . I wouldn't make it.

IAN: You did well. Just get your breath back for a minute.

BARBARA: I'm all right.

(*She breathes deeply for a few moments and then starts to edge along the ledge, face outwards. As the ledge gets narrower and narrower, she starts to panic.*)

BARBARA: Ian?

IAN: Oh, no, not that way. Now stay still. Give me your other hand. You've got to come back. Now . . . swing!

(IAN *reaches out his hand and pulls her back.*)

Now this time . . . face the rock. And reach . . . reach round with that arm.

(*She does so, but cannot find a handhold.*)

Reach higher . . . can you feel?

BARBARA: I . . . I can't reach it!

IAN: Higher, go on!

(BARBARA *stretches out desperately and, to her relief, manages to reach it.*)

BARBARA: Ah, yes!

IAN: Now . . . let go of my hand and . . swing yourself round. Go on . . . All right?

BARBARA: Yes.

KRISTAS: I'll throw the fire.

IAN: Right.

    (*He catches it.*)

IAN: Rope coming over!

KRISTAS: Will you go next, Antodus?

ANTODUS: No, you go on.

KRISTAS: Very well.

    (*He jumps over without difficulty.*)

IAN: You made it look easy.

    (*They untie the rope and* IAN *starts to coil
it once more.* KRISTAS *edges away round
the bend in the ledge.*)

Got the grip?

KRISTAS: Yes . . . I'm clear.

IAN: Rope coming over.

    (*He throws the coil across to* ANTODUS, *but*
ANTODUS *is so paralysed with fear that the
rope hits him and falls back down into the
chasm.* IAN *sees this and tries to make light
of it.*)

Sorry, bad throw, my fault! Move back from the
edge.

ANTODUS: I can't do it.

IAN: (*OOV*) Move back from the edge . . . and catch
this rope. Ready? Coming now!

    (*The sudden authority in* IAN's *voice
makes* ANTODUS *obey without thinking.
He catches hold of the rope.*)

Good. Now . . . tie it round yourself.

    (*As if in a trance,* ANTODUS *does as he is
told.*)

Tight! Now give yourself a good long run . . .
and jump! Ready whenever you are . . .

(*Still acting as if in a trance,* ANTODUS
*moves back away from the edge then,
screwing up all his courage, runs towards
the edge and jumps. He lands on the very
edge of the ledge, and losing his balance
topples backwards into the chasm.* IAN *at
once dives for the floor, but the shock of*
ANTODUS'*s full weight pulls him towards
the edge. He claws at the floor, but he is
dragged relentlessly towards the precipice.
From far below comes a strangled cry.*)

ANTODUS: (*OOV*) Help me! Help me!!

31. THE RAVINE.
(*At the end of the rope,* ANTODUS *swings
helplessly, unable to get a grip on the
smooth edge of the ravine.*)

ANTODUS: I can't hold on! I can't hold on!!

32. THE EDGE OF THE RAVINE.

(IAN *claws uselessly at the ledge as he
slides towards the edge of the ravine.*)

Next Episode:
THE RESCUE

EPISODE SEVEN

THE RESCUE

1. THE RAVINE (NIGHT).

(*At the end of the rope,* ANTODUS *swings helplessly, unable to get a grip on the smooth edge of the ravine.*)

ANTODUS: I can't hold on! I can't hold on!!

2. THE EDGE OF THE RAVINE.

(IAN *claws uselessly at the ledge, as he slides towards the edge of the ravine. Suddenly* GANATUS *is by* IAN's *side, desperately trying to stop* IAN *sliding further. The ledge beneath his feet crumbles and he nearly falls.*)

GANATUS: I daren't let go with my other hand.
IAN: Antodus! Get a grip on the rock-face. Take the weight off the rope!

3. THE RAVINE.

ANTODUS: It's too smooth!

4. THE EDGE OF THE RAVINE.

(GANATUS *is still clinging on to* IAN's *arm, but* IAN's *shirt begins to tear.* ANTODUS *is*

> *unable to gain a purchase on the smooth cliff-face and the rope is still bearing his full weight.)*

IAN: Stop it, you fool!

GANATUS: I'm losing you!

> *(IAN's hand begins to slip away from his grasp.)*

IAN: Sweat on my hands!

GANATUS: It's no good, Ian!

IAN: Call the others.

GANATUS: Kristas!

> *(There is no reply. IAN and GANATUS shout together.)*

Kristas!

IAN: Kristas!

5. *THE RAVINE.*

(ANTODUS reaches for his knife and starts to saw at the taut rope.)

6. *THE EDGE OF THE RAVINE.*

(Without warning, the rope goes slack and IAN, falls forward on to the ledge.)

GANATUS: Antodus!

> *(IAN pulls up the slack rope, and stares at the cut end in disbelief as slowly the bravery of ANTODUS's last act hits him. GANATUS stares blankly in despair, unable to accept what has happened.)*

7. *THE DALEK CONTROL ROOM.*

(*In an alcove,* THE DOCTOR *and* SUSAN *have been secured to a wall with metal clasps on their wrists and ankles.* THE DOCTOR *and* SUSAN *are arguing with a Dalek, and all three talk at once.*)

THE DOCTOR: You could live in the city and the others could . . .

SUSAN: There's room for both of you . . .

DALEK ONE: What we need for life, means death to the Thals.

THE DOCTOR: But why do you have to destroy? Can't you use your brains to try . . .

DALEK ONE: On-ly one race can sur-vive!

THE DOCTOR: What are you planning?

DALEK ONE: We wish to es-cape cap-tiv-it-y. Go out and re-build the Pla-net Ska-ro. Our ox-y-gen dist-rib-ut-ors will be be sub-ject-ed to waste ra-dia-tion by the ej-ect-or cap-sule.

THE DOCTOR: Nothing can live outside if you do that. Nothing!

DALEK ONE: Ex-cept the Da-leks.

(*A second Dalek is waiting silently nearby, with some sort of printed circuit held on its sucker-stick.*)

THE DOCTOR: When do you intend to put this into operation?

DALEK ONE: Now!

(*The Dalek takes the printed circuit from the other Dalek and glides over to the ejector capsule.*)

THE DOCTOR: This senseless, evil killing!

(*Unable to move,* THE DOCTOR *and* SUSAN *can only look at each other in despair.*)

8. THE TUNNEL.

(GANATUS, IAN *and* BARBARA *are huddled together.* KRISTAS *joins them.*)

KRISTAS: There has been a fall of rocks. The way is blocked.

IAN: Did you look all around it?

KRISTAS: Yes. There is no way through.

GANATUS: Then we'll have to go back. We've come this far. We've done our best . . . more. First Elyon died, and now my brother . . . for what? Can't you see there isn't any sense in it any more?

BARBARA: We can't give up now!

GANATUS: What is it that you want us to do?

IAN: We must go back and . . . find another way.

GANATUS: Why don't you just give up?

IAN: Because your brother died, for one thing. He gave us a chance.

GANATUS: My brother didn't want to come. He said we'd all die!

(*The light from the Thal's fire device suddenly dies.*)

BARBARA: What's the matter with it?

KRISTAS: I don't know. Dirt's got into it, I expect. Well, if we're going back we'll have to go back now. We can't cross the chasm without light.

BARBARA: Well, we still have the torch.

KRISTAS: That's weak, too.

IAN: Can we use it sparingly?

(KRISTAS *nods.*)

Well, turn it off, Kristas.

(KRISTAS *does so.*)

Right. Wait a minute . . .

(IAN *stands up.*)

There's a light coming in here. Where's it coming from? Where's the light coming from?

(*He realises that it is coming from just above their heads.*)

IAN: Here, give me a hand!

(*Together they pull away some loose rocks.*)

BARBARA: Can you see anything?

GANATUS: What is it?

(IAN *peers through the narrow gap and sees an enormous artificial cavern filled with pipes and what look like giant generators.*)

IAN: We're through! We must have been travelling under the pipes all the time. We're through!!

9. THE EDGE OF THE FOREST.

(DYONI *and the other Thals are still grouped at the edge of the forest.* DYONI *goes over to* ALYDON.)

DYONI: Alydon . . . the antenna hasn't moved for some time.

ALYDON: No. The Doctor must have succeeded in putting it out of action.

DYONI: But why haven't they returned?

ALYDON: The Daleks must have captured . . . Now, listen, everybody, the way to the city is clear, now is the time to attack!

(*He picks up a sturdy-looking branch.*)

We may be farmers, but have we forgotten how to fight?

(*Many of the other Thals also pick up weapons. One of them brandishes one of the metal claws from the magnadon creature.*)

10. *THE DALEK CONTROL ROOM* (*DAY*).

(THE DOCTOR *and* SUSAN *are still manacled to the wall as before. A Dalek is at the control panel.*)

DALEK ONE: Pow-er down to half.

DALEK TWO: Down to half.

DALEK ONE: Seal off Nuc-le-ar waste dis-pos-er.

DALEK TWO: Seal-ing comp-lete.

DALEK ONE: Be-gin ra-di-a-tion re-dir-ect-ion to dis-trib-ut-ion cap-sule.

(SUSAN whispers to THE DOCTOR.)

SUSAN: Can't we stop them? Can't we do anything?

(THE DOCTOR *speaks in a much louder voice.*)

THE DOCTOR: Just a moment! I haven't told you how we came to this planet.

DALEK ONE: It does not mat-ter now.

THE DOCTOR: But . . . but it does. I have a ship capable of crossing the barriers of Space and Time. Surely this would be invaluable to you?

DALEK ONE: A ship. What do you mean?

THE DOCTOR: A machine.

DALEK ONE: I do not be-lieve you.

THE DOCTOR:	But I have!
SUSAN:	It's true. We have!
DALEK ONE:	You are not cap-able of cre-at-ing such a mach-ine.
THE DOCTOR:	You took a part of my ship away from one of my companions, the young man.
DALEK ONE:	What did it look like?
THE DOCTOR:	A small rod with metal at either end. It belongs to my ship. A fluid link containing mercury. Examine it for yourselves. You will see it's part of a complicated machine.
DALEK ONE:	Yes, I have it here.

(*The Dalek glides over to another section of the control panel, where the fluid link has been placed.*)

THE DOCTOR:	Well, let me show you the Ship. Explain it to you. Help you to build another.
DALEK ONE:	A bar-gain for your lives?
THE DOCTOR:	Yes.
DALEK ONE:	Where is this mach-ine?
THE DOCTOR:	In the petrified forest. Outside the city.
DALEK ONE:	Good! When the neu-tron op-er-at-ion has been com-plet-ed, we will find a way to tra-vel out-side the ci-ty limits. We will ex-am-ine your mach-ine.
THE DOCTOR:	No, not unless you stop what you're doing! Otherwise I won't explain its secrets to you, and its philosophy of movement.
DALEK ONE:	Now we know of the mach-ine, we can ex-am-ine it for our-selves.
THE DOCTOR:	But you can't operate it without me.
DALEK ONE:	Eve-ry prob-lem has a so-l-ut-ion.

(*There is an urgent buzzing sound. The Dalek moves to operate the intercom.*)

DALEK: (*OOV*) Vi-brat-ion lo-cat-or re-cords move-ment in-side the ci-ty walls.

DALEK ONE: De-tails.

DALEK: (*OOV*) Dis-turb-ance is too great.

DALEK ONE: A-lert Da-leks in sect-ion one. The Thals are en-ter-ing the ci-ty.

SUSAN: Grandfather, they're coming!

THE DOCTOR: But can they get here in time?

11. A Corridor.

(IAN *makes sure the coast is clear and signals to* BARBARA, GANATUS *and* KRISTAS *to follow.*)

IAN: Now where are we?

BARBARA: No idea. I had some experience of these corridors. They all look alike.

IAN: Yes, we could go back to the lift, but . . . get back!

(*A Dalek appears at the other end of the corridor. The four dash back round the bend in the corridor. Before the Dalek can investigate, another Dalek voice comes over the intercom.*)

DALEK: (*OOV*) A-lert! The Thals are en-ter-ing the ci-ty. All Da-leks in sect-ion one to le-vel one. Im-med-iate! Im-med-iate!

(*The Dalek moves away out of sight. After a moment,* IAN *moves out of hiding.*)

IAN: Alydon and the Thals must be in the city. We must find the control room.

12. *The Dalek Control Room.*

(Again, a voice sounds over the intercom.)

DALEK: (*OOV*) Int-er-ior vid-eo-scopes are rec-ord-ing move-ments on le-vel eight.

(The Dalek in the Control Room operates another control and a picture of IAN *and* BARBARA *appears on a small view-screen.)*

SUSAN: Grandfather, look! Look, they found a way through!

DALEK ONE: All Da-leks on level eight. Ur-gent!

*(*IAN *appears on the screen again. He looks up directly at the screen, and then appears to reach out to it. Suddenly the picture vanishes from the screen. He has obviously broken the camera.)*

The Thals have pen-et-rat-ed to level eight. Im-med-iate ac-tion! Im-med-iate ac-tion!

DALEK TWO: How did they get in-to the ci-ty?

DALEK THREE: Cap-sule rea-dy to go cri-ti-cal!

DALEK ONE: Stand by!

DALEK THREE: Stand-ing by, rea-dy.

DALEK ONE: The last stage of the op-er-at-ion is a-bout to be-gin.

THE DOCTOR: Stop it, please . . .

DALEK ONE: Noth-ing can stop the Da-leks. Be-gin count-down. One Hun-dred.

DALEK THREE: Be-gin-ning now.

13. *A Corridor.*

*(*IAN *approaches with* BARBARA, *and* GANA-

TUS *and* KRISTAS *bring up the rear.* IAN
*reaches an intersection and suddenly,
without warning, a pair of hands shoots
out and grabs him. There is a brief
struggle before* IAN *recognises* ALYDON.)

GANATUS:	It's Alydon!
ALYDON:	Ganatus! Have . . . have you found the Doctor?
BARBARA:	Well, isn't he with you?
ALYDON:	No. He must have been captured by the Daleks, and Susan . . .
IAN:	But . . . the Daleks know you and the Thals are in the city.
ALYDON:	We split ourselves into groups, but without the Doctor we didn't know what to look for.
IAN:	We must find that control room!
BARBARA:	We must find the Doctor and Susan!
IAN:	Barbara, first and foremost we must find the control room and knock it out.

(ALYDON *and* GANATUS *have been quietly
talking.*)

ALYDON:	. . . and Antodus?
GANATUS:	Yes. He died bravely.

(*Suddenly another Dalek voice echoes out
of a nearby speaker.*)

DALEK:	(*OOV*) Da-lek group to con-trol room. Im-me-di-ate-ly. All Da-leks to le-vel ten.
ALYDON:	Well, this is level nine. We must be near.
KRISTAS:	We've got to go on.
BARBARA:	There's a lift back there. It's only one floor up.
DALEK:	(*OOV*) All Da-leks to le-vel ten im-me-di-ate-ly!

Cor-ri-dor in-ter-sect-ions on all le-vels oth-er than ten will be sealed now.

(*A door immediately behind the four begins to close.* GANATUS *dives to stop the door from closing, but he is too late. Another door to the side begins to close.*)

IAN: Kristas, help him! Get that one!

(*Again they are not quick enough to prevent the door from closing. The door in front of them also starts to descend.* KRISTAS *reaches it and struggles to hold it up, while* BARBARA *ducks under. As soon as she is through,* BARBARA *sees the next door beginning to close.*)

BARBARA: There's another one!
IAN: (*OOV*) Quickly, Barbara . . . get to it!

(BARBARA *runs to it and tries to hold the door up, but it is far too strong for her and it continues to descend.*)

Barbara!

14. THE DALEK CONTROL ROOM.

DALEK THREE: Fif-ty-two . . .
DALEK TWO: The Thals are block-ing the int-er-sect-ion from seal-ing on le-vel nine.
DALEK THREE: Fif-ty-one . . . Fifty . . .
DALEK ONE: In-crease po-wer! E-merg-en-cy! In-crease pow-er!
DALEK THREE: For-ty-nine . . . for-ty-eight . . .

15. A CITY CORRIDOR.

(BARBARA *is fighting a losing battle against*

the closing door. She is lying directly beneath it, but it is steadily crushing her. IAN *flings himself forward and* GANATUS *is with him.*)

IAN: All right . . .

(KRISTAS *and* ALYDON *appear.*)

IAN: Wait a minute, we'll take the strain . . . Barbara, try and slide yourself out.

BARBARA: I can't move.

(*The noise as the door strains to close increases in pitch.*)

GANATUS: They're pressing down harder.

IAN: They're increasing the pressure. Barbara, you must try and roll out. Try and free yourself!

KRISTAS: . . . just get my hands under . . .

(*With a final burst of strength,* KRISTAS *loosens the door's grip slightly and* BARBARA *squeezes through.*)

BARBARA: I'm, through!

IAN: Alydon, OK. Right, you go next!

(ALYDON *squeezes through the gap. The strain shows on* IAN'S *face.*)

16. THE DALEK CONTROL ROOM.

DALEK THREE: . . .ty-six . . . for-ty-five . . . for-ty-four . . .

(*A Thal runs through into the control room. A Dalek fires at him and he collapses, dead, on the floor.*)

for-ty-three . . . for-ty-two . . .

17. *The City Corridor.*

(*Only* IAN *remains on the wrong side of the door. He starts to squeeze underneath.*)

GANATUS: Hurry, Ian! It's crushing like stone.

IAN: Right.

(IAN *manages to squeeze out from under the door.* KRISTAS *and* GANATUS *release their grip and the door slams shut.*)

18. *The Dalek Control Room.*
(*The Dalek countdown continues.* THE DOCTOR *and* SUSAN *are still manacled to the wall as before.*)

DALEK THREE: For-ty . . . Thir-ty-nine . . . Thir-ty-eight . . . Thir-ty-se-ven . . . Thir-ty-six . . . Thir-ty-five . . . Thir-ty-four . . . Thir-ty-three . . .

(IAN *and the others can be seen at the far end of a corridor which leads directly to the control room.*)

Thir-ty-two . . . thi-rty-one . . .

(*A Dalek cuts across an intersection of the corridor;* IAN *and the others flatten themselves against the walls of the corridor.*)

Thir-ty . . . Twen-ty-nine . . . Twen-ty-eight . . . Twen-ty-se-ven . . . Twenty-six . . .

(*Once the Dalek has gone they gradually move up the corridor, getting nearer and nearer the control room.*)

Twen-ty-five . . . Twen-ty-four . . . Twen-ty-three . . . Twen-ty-two . . . Twen-ty-one . . . Twen-ty . . .

(IAN *and* ALYDON *catch sight of* THE DOCTOR *and* SUSAN, *then run over to try to free them.*)

Nine-teen . . . Eight-een . . . Sev-en-teen . . . Six-teen . . . Fif-teen . . .

(BARBARA *appears in the doorway. She throws a large rock at a Dalek. It strikes home but bounces off the Dalek's hard casing. At once the Dalek swings round and fires at* BARBARA, *who manages to duck out of the way.*)

Four-teen . . . Thir-teen . . .

DALEK ONE: Fol-low and kill her!

DALEK THREE: Twelve . . .

(BARBARA *and two of the Thals lasso a Dalek with the rope and manage to overpower it.*)

El-ev-en . . . Ten . . .

DALEK: Trapped! Help me! Trapped!

DALEK THREE: Nine . . .

(IAN *and* ALYDON *manage to undo the manacles and free* THE DOCTOR *and* SUSAN. *As they go to run away,* THE DOCTOR *collapses with cramps in his leg and a Dalek turns to fire at him.* IAN *throws something at the Dalek to distract it and* THE DOCTOR *bundles* SUSAN *out of the Dalek's fire.*)

Eight . . . Se-ven . . .

(*One of the Thals is riding on the back of a Dalek, desperately trying to cling on.*

> *Another Dalek shoots at him and he falls to the ground.*)

Six . . . Five . . . Four . . .

> (KRISTAS *swarms down a rope into the control room from above, but he is also shot by a Dalek. The injury is not fatal, however, and despite the pain, he manages to continue his attack on the Dalek.*)

DALEK TWO: Re-in-force-ments! Ov-er-pow-er-ed! Re-in-force-ments! Quick-ly!

> (GANATUS *jumps the Dalek from behind and, with a mighty push, sends it hurtling into the control console. There is a massive flash of light; at once the lights in the room dim.*)

THE DOCTOR: Chesterton, come here! Quickly!

IAN: Doctor! Doctor, I think they're dying!

DALEK ONE: Po-wer . . . go-ing . . .

THE DOCTOR: They were about to spread radiation into the air.

IAN: We've knocked out their source of power, I tell you. Look!

> (*He kicks the Dalek and it hurtles lifelessly across the room.* SUSAN *is by* KRISTAS'S *side.*)

SUSAN: Barbara, is he all right?

BARBARA: Yes, he's very badly hurt, but he's alive.

DALEK ONE: Lis . . . ten . . . to . . . me . . .

> (THE DOCTOR *goes over to the Dalek.*)

THE DOCTOR: Yes.

DALEK ONE: Stop . . . our . . . po . . . wer . . . from . . . wast
. . . ing . . . or it . . . will be . . . end . . . of the
. . . Da . . . leks . . .

THE DOCTOR: Even if I wanted to, I don't know how.

> (*The Daleks' sticks move very weakly now
> and, with a final groaning sound the
> sucker- and gun-sticks fall limply to the
> ground, while the eye-stick points straight
> upwards.* ALYDON *crouches beside the
> fallen body of one of his people.*)

ALYDON: It's finished. The final war. Five hundred years
of destruction end in this!

THE DOCTOR: No doubt you will have other wars to fight . . .
Chesterton, come along, my boy, we've got
work to do. I want to look at the reactors and
see if there is any radiation leakage.

IAN: Yes, and get the Ship working again, Doctor.

> (*He hands* THE DOCTOR *the fluid link.*)

THE DOCTOR: Hm? Oh yes, yes, yes, of course. Come along,
come along.

> (ALYDON *goes over to help* BARBARA *and*
> SUSAN, *who are supporting* KRISTAS *be-
> tween them.*)

ALYDON: Kristas, are you all right?

KRISTAS: Yes, thanks.

ALYDON: Let's get him up to the air. All this machinery –
what good is it to us? None of us knows the first
thing about it.

BARBARA: Well, you must experiment. These Dalek
inventions should be of some use to you.

> (THE DOCTOR, IAN *and* BARBARA *exit.*)

SUSAN: Yes, the Daleks have developed food by artificial sunlight. You've got everything you need now.

GANATUS: Yes, if only there'd been . . . some other way.

(SUSAN *and* GANATUS *exit. The inert forms of Daleks remain as a testament to what has happened.*)

19. THE FOREST CLEARING.

(ALYDON *is busy examining a piece of machinery salvaged from the Dalek City.* DYONI *is handing round small pieces of food to everyone. Carrying a rack of test-tubes,* THE DOCTOR *wanders over to* ALYDON *and chuckles softly to himself.*)

THE DOCTOR: This is what they call a compensator, my friend.

ALYDON: Which is?

THE DOCTOR: The whole of it. It's useless. Throw it away, forget it! Unless you want to live in a shell like our dead friends?

ALYDON: Oh . . . Where do you get your knowledge, Doctor? You know, there never seems to have been time to ask, but . . . we don't really know where you come from, or why . . .

(THE DOCTOR *ignores this question and continues as if it had never been asked.*)

THE DOCTOR: Rebuild a whole new world. Hm! How I envy you!

ALYDON: But you must stay and help us. We could learn from you.

THE DOCTOR: Oh no, no, no, no. I am afraid I am much too old to be a pioneer – although I was once, amongst my own people.

ALYDON: Well, then, stay and advise us. Please!

THE DOCTOR: No, no, thank you. We are much too far away from home, my Granddaughter and I. Thank you all the same, it's a nice gesture on your part. You know, this soil is not quite so barren as you think. I've been making tests, and even you might live to see and hear the birds amongst the trees. You wanted advice, you said – I never give it, never . . . but I might just say this to you. Always search for truth . . . My truth is . . . in the stars. And yours . . . is here.

(DYONI *comes over to them.*)

DYONI: Won't you rest with us?

THE DOCTOR: No, I'm afraid it's out of the question. But I might visit your grandchildren to find if they've learnt the secrets and if they have, well – who knows? I might live with them.

(*He chuckles to himself.* SUSAN *comes over. She is wearing one of the Thal's cloaks. It is much too big for her and covers her from head to toe.*)

SUSAN: Look, Grandfather! Isn't it terrific? Thank you Dyoni.

(*She trips over and starts to giggle.*)

IAN: What are you up to, Susan?

SUSAN: It's a present from Dyoni. Isn't it gorgeous?

IAN: It's lovely! Oh, by the way, Doctor, have you fitted the fluid link?

THE DOCTOR: Er, not yet. But I have it safely here and there's no need to worry about mercury, young man.

IAN: Good! Well, goodbye, Dyoni.

DYONI: Goodbye.

IAN:	Goodbye, Alydon.
ALYDON:	Goodbye, Ian.
THE DOCTOR:	Come along my child. I'm hungry.
SUSAN:	Goodbye, Dyoni. Thank you.
IAN:	Goodbye, Ganatus.
GANATUS:	Goodbye, Ian.
IAN:	Barbara?
BARBARA:	Right.
THE DOCTOR:	How stupid of me!

> (*He picks up the test-tube rack from on top of the Dalek compensator machine.*)

I very nearly forgot my specimens. Oh . . . Your hand, sir . . . Goodbye.

> (THE DOCTOR *goes to shake* ALYDON's *hand.* ALYDON *holds out his hand in return, slightly puzzled.* THE DOCTOR *shakes it firmly.*)

ALYDON: Goodbye, Doctor.

> (*A short way away,* BARBARA *and* GANATUS *are standing close together.*)

BARBARA: Well, Ganatus.

GANATUS: Well, Barbara. The dress you make from this won't be suitable for swamps and caverns, but . . .

> (*He hands* BARBARA *a length of material.*)

BARBARA: Well, that's a good thing.

GANATUS: Yes.

BARBARA: It's beautiful. Thank you very much. Thank you for everything.

GANATUS: I wish we . . .

(*Just then* SUSAN *pokes her head out of the
TARDIS.*)

SUSAN: Barbara, we're waiting!

(GANATUS *kisses* BARBARA *on her hand.
She responds by kissing his cheek, then
silently goes into the ship.* ALYDON *has
been quietly watching them and comes
over to* GANATUS.)

ALYDON: Come along, Ganatus.
DYONI: Don't be sad, Ganatus.
GANATUS: I won't be.

(*The sound of the TARDIS dematerialis-
ing rises above them.*)

I don't think I shall ever forget her.

(*Behind them the TARDIS fades from
sight.* DYONI *moves to the spot where it had
been and kneels on the ground in wonder-
ment.*)

20. INSIDE THE TARDIS.

(*The four travellers are grouped around
the control console.* THE DOCTOR *is busy
adjusting various controls. His practised
hands move swiftly over the various knobs
and switches. Suddenly, with no warning,
there is the noise of an explosion and a
bright flash of light. The four are all
thrown to the floor and the lights go out,
leaving the room in darkness . . .*)

Next Episode:
THE EDGE OF DESTRUCTION*

---

* This was the first episode of the next story, set entirely on board the TARDIS.

If you have difficulty obtaining any of the Titan range of the books and merchandise, you can order direct from **Titan Books Mail Order, 71 New Oxford Street, London, WC1A 1DG. Tel: (01) 497 2150**

The Tribe of Gum	£2.95
The Tomb of the Cybermen	£3.95
The Daleks	£3.95
Doctor Who Portfolio	£3.99

UK and Eire customers, please send a cheque or postal order.
For postage and packing: on orders up to £5 add £1.20; orders up to £10 add £2; orders up to £15 add £2.50; orders up to £20 add £2.70; orders over £20 add £3.
Overseas customers, please send International Bankers Draft in Sterling. For postage and packing (seamail) on orders up to £5 add £2; up to £15 add £3.50; up to £20 add £4; over £20 add 20% of total cost; airmail prices available by telephone.

Copies of the Titan Books Film and TV catalogue are available free with orders on request.

While every effort is made to keep prices steady, Titan Books reserves the right to change cover prices at short notice from those listed here and in the catalogue.